MW00715915

SAYING YES TO GOD

ESTHER

Other Studies in the *Women in the Word* Series

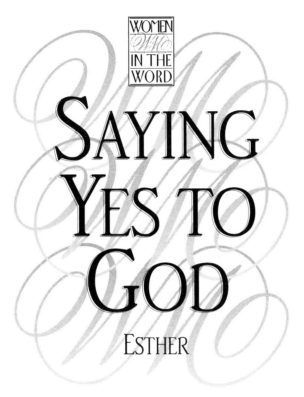

WOMEN
WHO
IN THE
WORD

SAYING YES TO GOD

ESTHER

Leader's Guide

Linda McGinn

Baker Books

A Division of Baker Book House Co
Grand Rapids, Michigan 49516

© 1996 by Linda McGinn

Published by Baker Books
a division of Baker Book House Company
P. O. Box 6287, Grand Rapids, MI 49516-6287

Printed in the United States of America

All rights reserved. No part of this publication may be reproduced, stored in a retrieval system, or transmitted in any form or by any means—for example, electronic, photocopy, recording—without the prior written permission of the publisher. The only exception is brief quotations in printed reviews.

ISBN 0-8010-5246-7

Scripture quotations are from the HOLY BIBLE, NEW INTERNATIONAL VERSION®. NIV ®. Copyright 1973, 1978, 1984 by International Bible Society. Used by permission of Zondervan Publishing House. All rights reserved.

CONTENTS

INTRODUCTION

Kari, a young mother of three under the age of five, hungers for the stabilizing influence she knows God's Word provides. She also wants to experience the comradeship and encouragement of others in her situation. A small group Bible study with friends held in her home seems ideal. But she's not a Bible teacher. Where is a Bible study anybody can lead, without any experience?

Mary, retired and widowed, searches for ways to reach out to the women in her community. How can she organize a Bible study? Who will lead them? Where can she find a study that enlivens God's Word for neighborhood friends who may never have read the Bible and that also offers content for church members who have studied the Bible for years?

Ellen's forty years of living leave her wiser to the things that really count in life. Her desire to know God more intimately and to study his Word mounts. She has been asked to consider organizing and teaching a large group Bible study—one that speaks to hearts as well as minds.

Women in the Word Bible study series can meet all of these needs. Several hundred women have used it in both small study groups and large group settings and have given helpful insight in the development of these leadership materials.

After deciding which type of group best fits your interests, skills, goals, and the local situation, use these tips to make your

Bible study one that others will seek out as a safe place for spiritual growth and personal development. These materials will help you move from your decision to begin a Bible study, to developing and continuing one that creates an environment for responsive participants.

PURPOSE

Women in the Word Bible studies are designed to meet needs unique to women. The goal is to provide teaching based on biblical passages and focused on topics relevant to women or the study of specific Bible books. It uses in-depth Bible study, small group discussion of God's Word as it relates to individual lives, and fellowship with one another.

The purpose is to grow in fulfilling God's command, "Let us hold unswervingly to the hope we profess without wavering, for He who promised is faithful. And let us consider how we may spur one another on to love and good deeds" (Hebrews 10:23).

While this study is usually a ministry, an integral part of the total church life, and is under the supervision of the church administration, it can often also be a community outreach program.

DESIGN

Women in the Word Bible studies are written to accommodate any small or large group Bible study. Three daily study questions enable a beginning or experienced student to spend varying amounts of time completing the lesson.

Questions may be answered quickly and concisely, yet they are written to stimulate further exploration as time allows. Cross-reference Scripture verses are often suggested for further investigation. Thought-provoking questions are raised for those familiar with the Bible, or for those who want to spend time reflecting on the topic being discussed.

The material is designed for a twelve-week session. However, the material can easily be adapted to fit local needs and situations.

FORMAT OPTIONS

1. You may best facilitate discussion among group members by developing a small group Bible study where every member contributes equally.
2. You may prefer to form and teach a small group study with a lecture format because you are the most trained and your instruction is the desire of the group.
3. You may want to combine the two options with small group sessions for discussion followed by a lecture period to summarize key points and add additional insights.

STEPS FOR PLANNING A STUDY

THE STARTING POINT: PRAYER

Every effective Bible study begins with prayer. Before any planning is done, contact eight to ten interested individuals and present the idea for a Bible study. Set a time for prayer and brainstorming—an open discussion of ideas concerning the formation of a Bible study. Ask individuals to pray in preparation for the meeting, and to come with ideas to consider.

Be prepared to share a key Scripture verse which you feel is relevant to your desire to develop such a study. This focus will help direct discussion. Begin with prayer asking God's direction and wisdom, recognizing his ownership over any newly begun Bible study and the need for his guidance so that his purposes will be accomplished with his glory as the driving motivation.

Continue, after prayer, with a free discussion soliciting any and all opinions for answering questions such as:

Who will attend the studies?
Who will find the studies appealing?
Which specific needs will be met through the Bible study?
Which setup (teacher, small group, lecture–small group combination) will be most effective?

Which *Women in the Word* study materials will be selected,
and by whom?
Who in the core group will be committed to future planning
and structuring of the Bible study?
When will the study begin, and where will it take place?

Ask for commitments. Decide how many of the women in
the core group are interested in forming the Bible study and
willing to be instrumental in its continued development and
maintenance. The core group's wisdom and that of other knowl-
edgeable advisors will continue to be essential to ensure success. The moment one person attempts to control or dominate
direction, God's ownership of the group is threatened. The
study may wither and die.

STEP TWO: KNOW YOUR GROUP MEMBERS

If your Bible study group is to survive, group leaders even-
tually will want to know the background, spiritual history, and
spiritual goals of each member. To begin with, however, there
are some key teaching principles that group leaders should use
if their leadership is to be effective . . . and welcomed by the
members.

Understanding the Adult Learner

1. Techniques used to instruct young people are not necessarily effective with adults.
2. Adults want to be included in planning sessions, leading
   to more vital and beneficial programs.
3. Involving adult learners in decisions motivates and stimulates them. They "own" or feel "invested" in the study
   when they take part in its direction and organization.
4. Helping the adult learner recognize needs should be a primary focus when planning the program. This facilitates
   personal application and causes an assimilation of the
   teaching that assures future involvement in the study. If
   adults do not recognize needs and personally apply the

material being studied, they will soon become disinterested in the material because "it's not relevant."
5. Learning focused on problem solving is most effective with adult students.
6. Drawing on adult learners' previous experiences enhances learning.
7. Encouraging adult participation by using ice breakers and group activities helps the individual to avoid embarrassment and a refusal to join in peer discussion and participation. Adults tend to take errors personally.
8. Instruction for adults should lead them to further personal study.

Keys for Successfully Teaching Adults

Research studies reveal that adults learn best when:

Dealing with specific life-changing events.
Reached at a "teachable moment" in their lives. This relates to recognizing when individual interest and motivation for study and change is at its highest point.
They have use for the knowledge or skill involved and can integrate it with what they already know. In most cases, learning is not its own reward.
Focus is on a single point.
The pace is slower and less complex. Fast-paced, complex, or unusual learning tasks interfere with the understanding of a concept.
New information is meaningful, includes helpful aids, and relates to previous knowledge.
The information agrees with the learner's values.
Projects are self-directed and self-designed. However, students do not want to be isolated. Some lectures and short seminars are encouraged.
How-to information and effective applications are used.
Expectations are clear.
Open-ended questions leading to discussion are a primary instructional method.

CREATIVE PARTICIPATION TOOLS

These tools can be used to involve participants in an interesting and inviting manner.

pantomime	videos
drawing	slides
charts	role play
testimonials	witnessing
competition	puzzles
debate	newspaper and
skits	magazine articles
panel discussions	research
question and answer	acrostic
sessions	cartoons, humor
personal experiences	posters
games	brainstorming
overheads	storytelling

STEP THREE: DEVELOP YOUR LEADERSHIP

Every woman is a leader. Whether or not you realize it, someone—husband, children, friends, fellow church members, or organizational coworkers—is looking to you as a role model or for direction in some area of life. A scary thought? It doesn't have to be. Your leadership is not dependent on you. It's dependent on God. Jesus makes that clear, "Apart from me you can do nothing" (John 15:5). It is Jesus' desire that his Spirit guide and direct your leadership. As you rely on Jesus, he will give you the power to be the leader he desires.

Qualities of an Effective Leader

Prayer comes first. Before taking any action, pray each day that God will provide the group members he has chosen. Ask him to be a unifying force undergirding you as you lead and encourage the group. Then trust him.

NEIGHBORHOOD BIBLE STUDY

The action of praying for God's choice of members and his unifying power is particularly significant when one begins a neighborhood Bible study. Considering the fact that attendees' various church backgrounds will reflect different theological positions, or no position, the issue of leadership becomes an important one.

Will you lead the study? This enables you to hold a more active position of resource person when difficult questions arise. This also allows you to maintain greater control over the direction of discussion when conflicts occur.

You may not feel comfortable in such a position and may choose to rotate leadership among participants. If so, it would be wise to allow each member to use the Leader's Guide when she prepares to lead the week's lesson. This provides theological continuity by suggesting answers to each question and gives confidence to the one who may feel intimidated by limited theological experience.

Whatever direction you choose for leadership, as always, dependence on the Holy Spirit is the key. You have the promise of James's words in James 1:5, "If any of you lacks wisdom, he should ask God, who gives generously to all without finding fault, and it will be given to him." God will guide your decisions as a group and honor your desire to learn more about his Word.

When questions and theological differences arise, go back to
your original premise. Everyone has met to learn more about
God's Word. No one but God has all the answers. We will be
learning more about his Word for the rest of our lives as we continue to seek his face. If you are unsure of the answer to a question, agree to discuss the issue with your pastor in the coming
week, promising to return with more information. You are
always encouraged to call a *Women in the Word* staff person
listed at the end of the chapter "Leading a Lecture–Small Group
Combination" for further insight on the subject.

LEADING A SMALL GROUP BIBLE STUDY

DEFINING THE GROUP LEADER'S ROLE

The small group leader is primarily a guide. Her role is to introduce the subject, guide the discussion, and encourage others to participate by interacting with Scripture. Allowing the Holy Spirit to direct according to the needs of each individual group member is the goal.

Small Bible discussion groups have proven to have a dynamic impact on those involved. Eager learners seek small groups because of their hunger for personal understanding of God's Word. Meeting with others also involved in satisfying this hunger creates an exciting environment for the discussion and study of God's Word.

Too often the purpose of discussion groups is misunderstood. They are not lectures or overlong dialogues by one member with another. They are not the vehicle for airing disagreements or arguments. A good discussion group provides a setting where learning, sharing, and discovery result as the members discuss biblical truth.

Through the Holy Spirit, God's Word can have a life-changing effect on the members of the group. The group leader recognizes that her role is simply to act as a guide, acknowledging that the Holy Spirit is the teacher and that the Bible is the reference book.

A successful small group Bible study:

Enables all members to describe their personal experiences. The opportunity to reflect on the ideas of others leads to further thoughts and insights.

Stimulates a spirit of love and acceptance that results in honest talk about problems, personal discoveries, searching questions, and individual needs.

Leads to the appreciation of each member that in turn builds confidence and freedom from the fear of embarrassment. Open discussion of the biblical message and its application becomes possible.

IDENTIFYING OBJECTIVES

A good leader knows that the first meeting is crucial. This means that planning, based on clear objectives, is the first work to be undertaken.

Identify in one or two sentences objectives for the first meeting. Clear objectives will help guide the discussion and focus the direction for questions. They are a map to be followed if the discussion goes off course into unrelated subjects. Clear objectives will help to evaluate progress during discussion so that necessary adjustments can easily and smoothly be made.

Write out objectives in understandable language and accompany them with a description of the desired outcome. For example, if the group is studying the twelfth chapter of Paul's first letter to the Corinthians, this might be written as an objective: Each member will be able to identify one specific God-given talent and describe how she can use it for the Lord and the building up of the body of Christ.

Next, develop a self-discovery statement to evaluate whether or not the objective has been accomplished. For example: Each member will plan to use her talent in a specific way. This would validate whether or not the objective was grasped by the members.

There may be times when your objectives may not be reached. Don't be disappointed. Reevaluate the objectives. They may need to be changed or rephrased. Remember that the Holy Spirit is the real director and he may have other plans for the group. Remain open to his leadership.

PREPARING FOR THE MEETING

Certain actions will take place at the first meeting. The group members will meet you and the other members. Their impressions of each other will affect and influence their participation throughout the study. Careful preparation is essential.

Begin by greeting each participant in a friendly, relaxed manner when she arrives. Always, always begin the meeting on time. Introduce yourself and give some information about your personal life (marital status, children, career, church activities).

Explain how the Bible study and related activities will proceed during each meeting.

(If you are one of several group leaders and the meeting is being held in a church, station a helper to give directions to the nursery as the women enter. In that situation, name tags are probably an excellent idea. Hand them out and request that women wear them regularly.)

Group members will react differently. Some may be new Christians while others may be more mature in their study and walk. A few members will be at ease, while others may be apprehensive and uncomfortable. Recognizing that anyone who feels unaccepted will probably not return, the leader should try to stimulate easy discussion with open-ended questions or statements that will help draw out even the shyest member.

Remember that the small group is a discussion group. The leader is not a director but a facilitator. The primary goal is to have every member participate in some way. An air of superiority can discourage an insecure member.

LEADING THE FIRST MEETING

Open with prayer. Discuss the objectives and introduce the Bible study. Begin with a discussion about the need for Bible study. Emphasize that all Christians need spiritual food, fellowship, and training. Explain that members should not only seek to be fed but also should learn to feed themselves, a basic requirement of a mature Christian.

State the three basic questions about Scripture that are incorporated in every *Women in the Word* daily lesson. What does it say? What does it mean? How can it be applied? Assure the group that the questions in the study section are intended to stimulate thinking. They are not intended to make anyone feel belittled or ignorant of God's Word.

Stress that Bible study in small groups should lead to friendly discussion and to further understanding and discovery of Bible facts. The purpose is to get to know the Bible and the person of Jesus Christ.

Introduce the first lesson. Give the members about five to ten minutes to work on a few of the first questions. Then ask the group to share answers.

Questions are valuable. Three types of questions used by most leaders include discovery, understanding, and application. Clear and relevant discovery questions determine the discussion topic and response received. Responses should stimulate participation and discussion.

The understanding type of question encourages group members to go beyond initial observation. They should open up, deepen, illustrate, or clarify the discussion. The goal is to help the group understand the meaning of the discovered truth.

The aim of application questions is to stimulate group members to act. Discovery and understanding should naturally lead to application.

Be discreet when you ask an application question. Some members will be excited about the changes in their lives and want to share. Others will need time to evaluate their progress. Be aware, however, that application questions are the link between Bible study and daily living.

As a leader, strive to be an encourager. If someone seems to have arrived at an incorrect answer, try to correct it through group discussion and a different approach to the solution.

Always guard members from embarrassment and discourage any type of derision or ridicule. If you feel there is a serious misunderstanding, talk with the person in a one-to-one meeting.

End the meeting on time. Make this a regular pattern. Remind the group of the date, time, and place of the next meeting. You may want to adopt the pattern of closing the meeting with conversational prayer but unless you are certain most of the group members are comfortable with conversational prayer, it is best for you to give the closing prayer at the first meeting.

INTRODUCING SMALL GROUPS TO CONVERSATIONAL PRAYER

Many church members seldom or never pray aloud in a church group. It can prove to be an embarrassing, discouraging experience for some. "I sound so stupid." "I can't think of the right words to say." "I don't know the lingo."

However, praying together is essential in a discussion group. Experience will eliminate the fears of those who are uncomfortable with group prayer. The leader is the one who demonstrates that praying as a group can be a unique worship experience, not something to dread.

When introducing the session for conversational prayer, remind the members that form is not important. There is no right or wrong way to talk with the Lord. There are no special words. God listens to all prayers, however worded. Do not pressure anyone to pray. In time, the familiarity and encouragement of the group may provide the needed impetus.

You, the leader, should pray first. Ask a member to make the final prayer. Be brief. Introduce special concerns and requests. Trust the Holy Spirit to continue the circle of prayers. Pray spontaneously, not in any sequence. Pause long enough to allow others to add their thanks, praise, or requests.

HANDLING PROBLEMS IN A GROUP

At times conflicts may arise. Disagreement may come from misguided opinions, pettiness, or false doctrines. This may happen in an otherwise harmonious group because of a difference of opinion or interpretation of a Bible passage.

If the atmosphere in the group is generally relaxed, strong disagreements are unlikely to develop. But if a situation does arise, it is the leader's responsibility to try to "calm the waters." One approach is to direct the group to search God's Word to uncover answers that will relieve tension and arrive at a solution. Then summarize the discussion for clarity and resolution. That approach implies that the leader has a thorough knowledge of the Scriptures or has instant access to a concordance that will help to pinpoint relevant verses on the same topic.

If disagreement persists, it would be wise to agree to wait until the next meeting, seek outside information on the topic or issue, and further discuss the issue at that time. You may present several positions of belief then, making clear that holding differing beliefs is fine as long as Scripture is not contradicted. There are several ways to view many passages of Scripture.

Other conflicts that may arise include the talkative member who dominates the discussion or introduces extraneous subjects. Here you must quietly, skillfully bring the discussion back on track. "This is interesting. However, we have left our topic. Perhaps we can get back to that later."

Sometimes an incorrect answer will be offered. Never tell a member that an answer is wrong. Instead, shift the discussion to someone else and ask for an opinion.

Develop your own style of handling other unforeseen problems. Every group is different and each seems to have an individual personality. Begin by praying that God will speak through his Word so the group will be led to realize his truth. Know the passage to be studied, be excited about the group, their discoveries, and the opportunity to lead them. Remember to relax and use humor when appropriate. You can conduct a study, under the Holy Spirit's direction, that will be an inspiration to all.

AVOIDING LEADERSHIP TRAPS

Be careful about comparing yourself to others. Each person is unique with distinct God-given abilities and strengths. "We do not dare to classify or compare ourselves with some who commend themselves. When they measure themselves by themselves, . . . they are not wise" (2 Corinthians 10:12).

Avoid becoming discouraged. At times you may find the discussion unfocused or unproductive. By searching for obstacles and reasons for failure, you will be alert to ways of improving your leadership. This will help you grow as a leader. Be encouraged because God is honored when his Word goes out.

Don't give up. Remain committed to the completion of the study. Keep your goals in mind. Trust that if it is God's will, the study will prosper.

LEADING A LECTURE–SMALL GROUP COMBINATION

Combining a small group and lecture format is becoming an increasingly effective vehicle for teaching God's truth and for attracting those who are not usually comfortable in a traditional church setting.

Large groups are best implemented when three or four small groups of ten to twelve participants can be formed. This format can accommodate hundreds of women so there are unlimited opportunities for expansion.

Small group studies grow to large ones after the structure and organization is in place and public invitations are extended. Enthusiastic recruitment by excited potential members often brings in other women. Newspaper and radio advertisements positioning the Bible study as a community opportunity bring many who feel less threatened in a public setting.

Several assistants, in addition to the discussion leaders, will be needed as the group expands: teacher's assistant, worship leader, and children's program assistant.

The lecture–small group format is primarily teacher-driven. Because most effective teaching methods stimulate group involvement, it is imperative that the teacher implement techniques that incorporate the group. Even if you have been selected to teach because of your previous training and expertise, search for specific and original methods to assure that all mem-

25

bers will be encouraged to participate. You may find the material about knowing your group members (pp. 12–13) helpful.

RESPONSIBILITIES OF LECTURER

1. To present a weekly lecture that has as its goal an accurate summary of the biblical content of the lesson with careful attention given to the application to a woman's life. Scripture states that a teacher of biblical truth is held accountable by God for what is presented. Therefore, the lecturer must plan enough time in her schedule for conscientious study of the material to be presented.
2. To meet with the discussion group leaders and other assistants on a regular basis as often as necessary to ensure a smoothly run class.
3. To help select the following year's leadership team.
4. To help plan the following year's study.
5. To report information about the study to the church administration.
6. To remain available for consultation, questions, and small group activities as appropriate.

RESPONSIBILITIES OF TEACHER'S ASSISTANT

1. To set up main auditorium and group meeting rooms.
2. To work with the secretary on group lists with names, addresses, and phone numbers of all attendees.
3. To be a spiritual support for leaders and assistants as needed.
4. To be the representative between the study group and the church administration.
5. To assist in the recruitment of group leaders and assistants.
6. To record weekly attendance and donations.
7. To write necessary thank-you notes.

RESPONSIBILITIES OF WORSHIP LEADER

1. To plan a fifteen-minute period of worship primarily focused on group singing but possibly incorporating brief

testimony, relevant quotes, anecdotes, or mini-drama to introduce the week's lesson.
2. To distribute songbooks or provide overhead transparencies or song sheets so words for all songs are accessible.
3. To work closely with the teacher-lecturer on ongoing plans for study.

RESPONSIBILITIES OF CHILDREN'S PROGRAM ASSISTANT

1. To offer spiritual support to program workers.
2. To schedule hours for paid and volunteer workers.
3. To assist teachers with lessons and crafts, if needed.
4. To help select children's program curriculum. Excellent material is available from Honey Word, P.O. Box 25189, Colorado Springs, CO 80936 (1-800-466-3996).
5. To listen to and mediate any problems.
6. To represent the children's program and report to the teacher's assistant.
7. To help prepare reports to church administration.
8. To assist in setting up, assigning space, and cleanup.
9. To recruit new workers as needed.
10. To make certain that refreshments (crackers and juice) are available in the nursery.

RESPONSIBILITIES OF DISCUSSION LEADER

1. To guide the group's discussion to discover the truth as outlined in the lesson.
2. To be an encourager to the group members, not a lecturer or counselor.
3. To view the group members as being placed in the group by God.
4. To be in prayer for each of the women in the group on a regular basis. To let each member know she is being remembered in prayer. To encourage each member in her personal prayer life.

5. To make personal contact with anyone who doesn't know the Lord, attempting to share the gospel at an appropriate time.
6. To be personally committed to the study of the Word.
7. To help each group member to establish a consistent habit of Bible study. To encourage them to complete the lessons. To phone them during the week, asking for prayer requests, and making note of answered prayer.
8. To initiate monthly luncheons for fellowship and spiritual growth.

Guidelines for Discussion Leaders

The leader's main job is to be an encourager. The most important form of encouragement is the art of listening. This should be one of your primary goals as a Discussion Leader. Listening takes concentration, energy, and practice. Ask God to help you be open to growing in this very important skill.

Strive to guide the group's discussion to discover the truth outlined in the written lessons.

1. Rephrase the discussion questions to clarify them.
2. Allot a suggested time for answering each question to assure completion of the study and to motivate the members to complete all the questions.
3. Start the discussion promptly.
4. Stay with the study and save unrelated questions for a private conversation.
5. Stress the importance of stating Bible references and having answers in a written form.
6. Recommend that members stay in the Scripture passage found in the study.
7. Allow volunteering.
8. Occasionally, when the class seems unsure of an answer, the leader may want to give a response.
9. Strive to listen carefully to answers, using brief responses such as: valid point, hadn't thought of that, I can tell you studied, helpful illustration, answer shows insight, to the

point, good observation, beautifully expressed, thank you, God is great.

10. Wrong answers should be treated graciously. Some responses might be: Could we say more about this question? I'd be interested in the findings of others. Does someone else have something to say about this?

11. Try to draw out the truth when dealing with a partial truth answer. Then you can restate the complete truth.

12. Salvation questions may come up during the discussion time. If the class member seems to be unclear about her salvation, you may wish to say, "What does the Bible say about this?" If it should come up, but is not a question in the lesson, arrange to talk with her later. It is usually wise to have a gospel tract available to share.

13. Make every effort to refrain from making negative comments about any church or organization. Guests may come from all walks of life, seeking the truth. You are the model God has placed in your group.

Developing Listening Skills

Every Discussion Leader will benefit from developing better listening skills. Many people lack listening skills because our listening attention spans have decreased. Because of the constant noise of contemporary life, many of us can actively listen for only a few minutes. But we can improve.

God thinks listening is important. The word *listen* occurs 352 times in the Bible. The word *listening* is found eighteen times.

These steps will help a Christian make listening the doorway to loving.

1. Seek silence. Turn off the TV and radio. Attend to the sound around you.

2. When someone speaks, be discerning. Consider the feelings and intentions of the speaker.

3. If you doubt the meaning of the spoken words, reword and say what you understand. "If I understand you correctly, you are saying . . ."

4. Be accepting without making value judgments before the speaker has finished.
5. Make a conscious effort to concentrate on both the words and meaning.

Planning Monthly Luncheons

Fellowship is an integral part of *Women in the Word* ministry. Informal monthly luncheons provide the atmosphere for meaningful and encouraging interaction between the women who meet weekly in their small groups. (These ideas may easily be adapted to evening suppers for women who attend classes at night.) These suggestions may help you plan these luncheons.

1. Announce plans at discussion group meeting, giving date, location, and type of luncheon.
2. Solicit volunteer hostesses who will provide a meeting place, beverages, and dessert.
3. If needed, provide extended child care so only nursing infants will accompany mother.
4. Write thank-you note to hostess immediately following luncheon.
5. Decide on luncheon menu:

   Brown-bag—each member brings piece of fruit and sandwich. Sandwiches are quartered and fruit is cut up for salad.

   Salad variety—each member brings her favorite luncheon salad.

   Large tossed salad—each member brings an assigned ingredient.

   Hero sandwich—each member brings an assigned ingredient.

   International, one-country, or style of cooking. Each member brings her favorite luncheon dish.

6. Subtly yet intentionally guide the discussion at the luncheons. Talk about people or a special book that influenced

the spiritual life of the women at the luncheon. Discuss methods of modeling a life of prayer. Reflect on a childhood memory about how God worked in a young life. Questions not pertaining to the lessons or needing research that lend themselves to a relaxed setting can be discussed.

PREPARING FOR FIRST MEETING

After job descriptions have been completed and all positions filled, it is time to prepare for the first meeting. The core group of interested women has met and prayed for several months. Meetings with leaders have been held, supplies have been purchased, meeting rooms assigned. Personal contacts and newspaper and radio advertisements have generated a list of women registered for the first session. Each has been placed in a designated small group and has been contacted and welcomed by the group leader.

Discussion Leaders are given the suggested time schedule and are asked to review "Guidelines for Discussion Leaders" in preparation for the first meeting. They also receive "First-Day Class Instructions."

SUGGESTED TIME SCHEDULE

Morning	Evening	
9:15–10:00 A.M.	6:15–7:00 P.M.	Discussion leaders meet with teacher for a time of prayer, questions to be clarified concerning the week's study, and general discussion.
10:00–10:15	7:00–7:15	Worship time for singing and focusing group on the person of Jesus Christ and the character of God in preparation for the lecture and discussion.
10:15–11:00	7:15–8:00	Lecture by teacher, highlighting the week's study material.
11:00–12:00	8:00–9:00	Small group (10–12 women) discussion time for sharing answers to the daily questions.

FIRST-DAY CLASS INSTRUCTIONS

1. Have the room set up ahead of time.
2. Prepare a name tag for each woman.
3. Pray before the class session that the Lord will enable you to be friendly, relaxed, and to have a quality of leadership graced with love and dignity.
4. Introduce yourself and briefly tell something about your family status, career, church membership.
5. Pass out the name tags and ask women to wear them to all the meetings.
6. Ask class members to introduce themselves and tell something about their family status, career, church membership. (As an alternative allow about five minutes for class members to discover one interesting fact about each member, using clues that you have written out after talking with each one. Example: Has a daughter serving as a missionary nurse in Sri Lanka. Has recently retired after teaching third-graders for forty years. Has moved three times in five years. This allows even the shyest member to participate without feeling intimidated.)
7. Talk about the general guidelines for the study as explained in the information sheet (see pp. 35–36). Explain the question-discussion page.

   The guidelines are intended to draw all class members into a disciplined, daily prayer and in-depth study of Scripture. They enable the women to be prepared to share in the discussion time.

   Each step of the study process is a preparation to build on information: first from personal Bible study, then from the lecture, and finally from group discussion.
8. Relax. Don't worry about catching all the slips the first day.
9. Inform the group members that any Bible version is acceptable. Different translations may make a slight difference in their answers.

Maintaining a Successful Bible Study

Continued prayer and the joint counsel of your leadership team will enable you to evaluate questions and concerns as your study develops. This ensures reasonable solutions and adjustments. Remaining attentive to the Holy Spirit's direction means a willingness to modify any program to improve it and meet any existing or evolving needs.

Be alert. Identify weak areas that can be strengthened. Appreciate those who have contributed to the strength of the program and invite their suggestions. Constantly remember that God holds ownership of the Bible study. The leadership team yields constantly to his direction. His glory is the ultimate goal.

Keeping in step with the Holy Spirit is the key to an effective and prosperous ministry so that many may come to know Jesus Christ more intimately through the gateway of God's Word.

Now you are ready to begin your adventure with God as he reveals his will and as his plan unfolds the Bible study he has in mind.

For more information, supplementary resource materials, and audio tapes concerning the formation and maintenance of vibrant, effective, small and large group Bible studies, please contact:

Roz Soltau
Women in the Word
   Ministries
(954) 782-7506

Karen Vander Elzen
Living in the Word International
P.O. Box 8998
Asheville, NC 28814
1-800-948-0745 or
(704) 645-5115

CLASS MEMBER INFORMATION

This Bible study is designed to meet needs unique to women by using in-depth Bible study, small group discussion of God's Word as it relates to individual lives, and fellowship with one another. Our purpose is to extend God's kingdom in a woman's life, home, church, community, and throughout the world.

GENERAL GUIDELINES

1. Please come to class each week with written answers to the question-discussion page, and a Bible version of your choice. Many excellent Bible translations are available. Our recommendation list includes the New International Version (NIV), the King James Version (KJV), and the New American Standard (NASB).
2. In your home study, remember that prayer is vital to understanding any portion of Scripture. Ask God to help you. You may not always understand the Bible's meaning. Don't be discouraged. We are given a lifetime to understand. Be patient and as you continue searching Scripture, God, through his Holy Spirit, will reveal his truths. When reading, ask God to make his Word personal and interesting. Ask yourself: What does it say? What does it mean? What does it mean to me? How can I apply it personally?

3. A disciplined study time is important. Be prepared and willing to set aside a daily prayer-study time. Make time for God and his Word and hold on to it. With God's strength and help you will discover your best time of day, whether it be morning, afternoon, evening, or simply your child's nap time. Don't feel guilty if finding the time is difficult. Ask God to help you. He will.

4. The study lesson is divided into five days for your convenience. Each day read the Scripture passage. In the space provided answer as many questions as possible. Pray concerning any particular thought or lesson that may apply to your personal life, understood from this portion of God's Word. Do not be discouraged by what you may not understand. Skill and understanding in answering the questions will develop with experience.

5. You are encouraged to dig deep in your personal study of Scripture. You may want to use a concordance to look up other passages related to a word or words of particular interest to you, but you are encouraged to delay referring to Bible commentaries until you have completed the question-discussion page. This procedure will allow you to discover your own insights.

6. Sharing time in individual discussion groups offers an opportunity to explore more than one answer to a question. It is most beneficial to give the Bible reference from which your answer came. Be careful not to monopolize the discussion and to allow other members to participate.

LESSON AIMS
AND ANSWERS

SETTING THE STAGE FOR ESTHER

Esther's story begins in 483 B.C., 103 years after Nebuchadnezzar captured the Jews and 55 years after Zerubbabel led the first group of exiles back to Jerusalem under Cyrus's decree. Esther lived in the kingdom of Persia, formerly called Babylon, and as a Jewish exile found great freedom there. Many of her people remained in Persia even after their freedom to return to their homeland was secure. They may have feared the dangerous journey. Some refused to abandon their successful businesses.

King Ahasuerus, better known by his Greek name Xerxes the Great, was Persia's fifth king. His winter palace was in Susa, where the story takes place. A Jewish orphan, Esther was raised by her cousin Mordecai. At the request of the king's commissioners, she was chosen to compete for the title of Queen.

Recorded in story form, the Book of Esther excites the reader as each chapter ends with a cliff-hanger that builds the suspense. Though authorship of Esther is unknown, it seems clear that a Jew penned the historical commentary. The earliest possible date for the book's authorship is considered to be 460 B.C., and it seems conclusive that the book was written before the Persian empire fell to Greece in 331 B.C.

Besides King Xerxes and Esther, two characters dominate the narrative: Haman and Mordecai. Haman was a chief official in Persia. Because the king and his officials were considered divine, Haman grew to despise Mordecai because he was unwilling to yield to Haman's demand for worship. Mordecai, a Jew, refused to worship or attribute divine value to any but the one true God. Mordecai would not even consider kneeling before Haman in an act acknowledging him as a god.

Haman was an Agagite which proves most interesting in light of the fact that Agag was the king of the Amalekites. Since Moses' day the Jews and Amalekites remained bitter enemies. According to biblical history, Agag, king of Amalek, attacked Israel after the exodus. In response God commanded that the Israelites kill every Amalekite. Destroy all that were captured and seize no plunder, commanded God. After their victory over the Amalekites, Saul, king of Israel at the time, disobeyed God. He allowed his army to plunder. Also, he permitted King Agag to live. For these sins, Saul lost his kingship. Yet, five hundred years later in the palace of Xerxes, God allowed the descendent of Agag, Haman, to confront the descendent of Saul, Mordecai, in a battle to death. By this he gave Israel a second opportunity to obey his Word.

One author writes, "The Book of Esther continues to be the number one favorite with Jewish communities, and is read in the family every year at Purim, as has been the traditional custom through the centuries." Though God is not mentioned in the text, his powerful and victorious intervention in the lives of his people and in the events of history cannot be denied. God reigns and his purposes will be accomplished. The book's theme is spoken by Mordecai to Esther, "If you remain silent at this time, relief and deliverance for the Jews will arise from another place, but you and your father's family will perish. And who knows but that you have come to royal position for *such a time as this*" (Esther 4:14, emphasis added).

As you study this fascinating book, identify the characteristics of God as he orders and directs the lives and circumstances of history for the benefit of his people and the glory of his name.

ESTHER 1

The stage is set. Queen Vashti displeases the king, loses royal position, and her replacement is sought. Learning to say yes to God by being a woman of God, while understanding God's protective plan for biblical submission, headship, and authority is the focus. How can you find fulfillment in your role as a woman, a wife, a mother? Unearth new insights imbedded in this fascinating narrative.

LECTURE SUMMARY

In chapter 1, the first issue to be discussed is that of "understanding the times." In every generation each culture holds certain presuppositions which determine the way people think and live. When we identify the presuppositions of our culture, we know the most effective ways to present the gospel's Good News. We will see that Xerxes' advisors understood the times enough to recognize the implications of Vashti's disobedience. Mordecai understood the times and so he demanded that Esther conceal her Jewish heritage. We need to be wiser than Vashti as we seek to understand the times in which God has placed us so that we may learn how to best communicate the gospel to a hurt and dying world.

The issue of submission is discussed next. Much about this topic is included in the chapter answers but summary comments seem appropriate. God places those in authority over us for our protection. When we yield to the leadership of another we are able to do so by first yielding to God's sovereign care in all things. His authority acts as the ultimate authority to which we yield. His care umbrellas our lives, protecting and insuring that all things touching us are being worked out to accomplish his perfect will for us.

Concerning submission, one author writes, "What submission is not: We have talked about what submission is, but now we need to see what it is not. It does not mean that the one in authority is smarter that I am, more intellectual, more able, more talented, more experienced, better equipped, or more important. It does not mean that the one in authority is a dictator. It does not mean I should not offer the full extent of my knowledge, advice, or participation. It definitely does not mean that the one in authority has a greater value in God's sight than I, or is loved any more or is any more spiritually mature necessarily. It simply means for the specific task, time, or place, God has ordained that someone be the Leader."

The Deity is the ultimate example of authority and submission. In 1 Peter 3:22 Christ "has gone into heaven and is at God's right hand—with angels, authorities and powers in submission to him." This is where the Father placed him. And Jesus sends the Holy Spirit, according to John 15:26, to indwell the believer. The three persons of the Godhead, Father, Son, and Holy Spirit are equal in value yet different in function. God initiates, Jesus responds to do the Father's will, and the Holy Spirit fulfills Christ's work among us. All are the same in character and attribute, yet different in activity.

The final issue is that of a wife's responsibility to act with respect toward her husband as unto the Lord. We see that disrespect can be a stumbling block to those who await a godly example, and we learn that true respect is showing regard and esteem toward another.

━━ DAY 1

1.   **Read Esther 1.**

       As if you were writing a play, list the facts that set the stage for the drama that is about to unfold (Esther 1:1–8).

Xerxes rules over 127 provinces from his royal throne located in Susa.

He decided in the third year of his reign to hold a banquet for all his nobles and officials including the military leaders of Persia and Media, the princes, and the nobles.

For 180 days he displayed the wealth and splendor of his kingdom.

The banquet that followed lasted seven days for all those present in Susa.

The king sent the eunuchs who served him to bring his beautiful wife Vashti in her royal crown to meet his guests. She refused.

Xerxes burned with anger and spoke with his advisors concerning an appropriate response to the refusal. "The queen's conduct will become known to all women, and so they will despise their husbands. . . . This very day the Persian and Median women of the nobility who have heard about the queen's conduct will respond to all the king's nobles in the same way. There will be no end of disrespect and discord."

Vashti was commanded never again to enter the presence of the king.

The king issued an edict that every man should be ruler over his household.

2.   (a)   What do we learn about King Xerxes from this passage (Esther 1:1–8)? List facts.

The king ruled a vast domain (verse 1).

The king was proud of his possessions (verse 4).

The king was rich (verses 6–7).

The king was generous (verse 7).

The king drank (verse 10).

The king considered his wife a possession (verse 11).

The king considered his wife beautiful (verse 11).

The king became furious and burned with anger when he was disobeyed (verse 12).

(b) How do the following verses shed light on Esther 1:4–7?
Proverbs 11:2

Proverbs 29:23

Isaiah 42:8

Mark 7:20–23

Pride was a driving force in the king's attitudes and actions. Disgrace, humiliation, reproof by God, and evil are results of pride.

3.   **Read and reflect on 1 John 2:15–17.**
    (a) What meaning does verse 17 have for you today?
    Pride, a promotion by the world, is worthless eternally while the will of God holds eternal value.

    (b) Ask God to identify any areas in your life that reflect a greater love for the world than for him. Surrender these areas to God so that he can give you a greater love for himself and his kingdom.
    Personal response

══ DAY 2

4.   **Read Esther 1:9–12.**
    (a) Who was in attendance at Queen Vashti's banquet?
    The women in the royal palace

    (b) How was Vashti's behavior a negative testimony to others?
    Refusing to obey her husband's request displayed a lack of respect and regard for her husband. Doing so in front of all the women in the palace created a negative example for them.

5.   (a) What was the king's request?
    That she appear in her royal crown for all to see.

(b) Was his request indecent or ungodly?

Not that we are aware

(c) Has your husband ever asked you to make an appearance at a business or social function?[*]

Yes

(d) How does it show your love and respect for your husband to comply even if you don't want to do something he asks?

If his request is neither ungodly nor immoral, it shows a simple regard for him as a person. Respect his request and comply as a sacrificial act of love. In a marriage either partner may be asked by the other to do something that does not particularly interest or excite him or her, but before refusing the request out of selfish indifference it would be wise to consider if refusal would hurt the mate unnecessarily.

(e) How does it reflect Christ's unselfishness, as seen in Philippians 2:5–8?

Jesus gave of himself for us, sacrificially thinking of us first to the point of death on a cross. Our attitude should exemplify the same sacrificial love. Our human nature makes that impossible. We are unable to demonstrate selfless love. But the Holy Spirit of God makes it possible because his power can accomplish it. "Each of you should look not only to your own interest, but to the interests of others." Concerning our behavior toward others we are encouraged to follow Jesus' example.

6. (a) Read these passages and explain how they relate to this section of Scripture.

1 Peter 3:1–7   The term *submission* has been grossly misunderstood by many in the Christian community. It has been distorted to represent an oppressive control of one individual over another, a tool for manipulation, and a means to force

---

[*] If you are a widow, set a godly example for younger women by sharing an example from your marriage of obedience to the principles discussed in these questions.

another to be subservient against his/her will or desire. This is not biblical submission.

Hupotasso is the Greek military term for submission. One individual surrenders to the will of another not because one individual has more personal value than the other, but simply because it is the function of the leader to hold the final responsibility for decisions made as well as their ultimate consequences. In a marriage, this responsibility falls to the man. (*Submission* stands in opposition to the term *subservient* because subservience pertains to slaves and infers a slaving, or cringing, spirit. This is *not* an aspect of biblical submission.)

He is held ultimately responsible for all decisions he and his wife make and for their consequences. Submission within a marriage is a choice. It is the choice to joyfully submit to the leadership of the other.

As we read in Ephesians 5:21, in marriage, the mutual and personal value of each is recorded before any leadership positions are delineated. "Submit to *one another* out of reverence for Christ." In mutual submission the attitude of each is one of respect and love. This is established before the actual duties of each are defined.

In decision making, after husband and wife have an opportunity to discuss an issue and attempt to genuinely understand each person's point of view in order to decide fairly, the husband then holds the responsibility for whatever decision is made. How can a wife trust her husband's decisions? She cannot. He is human, fallible, and apt to make mistakes just as she. But she can trust God who is supernatural, omniscient, and all-powerful to work through any and all decisions to work his will and accomplish his best for their lives.

When you prayerfully obey God's word and choose to yield yourself to the decisions of a husband, godly or ungodly, you can be assured that it is in God's hands where you place your care, and those hands never fail or falter. At the same time God never expects you to obey your husband's request if it specifically and directly violates God's word. Your first obedience is to Christ and only as you submit to his leadership can you then submit to the leadership of another.

Ephesians 5:21–33   After establishing mutual submission in verse 21, God goes on to describe the active participation of both husband and wife in the daily functioning of marriage. An umbrella of protection is described in this passage. Christ first submits to the Heavenly Father and then man submits to Christ. Like man, woman first submits to Christ then to the leadership of man.

Submission does not deal with value because then it would appear that God the Father was greater than his Son Jesus Christ which we know is false. Submission deals with rank and function. Though Father and Son are both God, equal in value, the Son submits to the Father's direction and leadership in the same way that the wife submits to her husband.

In this particular passage, women are directed to maintain a gentle and quiet spirit so as to win the unbelieving man to the Lord. This is not speaking of a personality quality of quietness. This speaks of a spiritual attitude. Dwelling in God's peace that passes all understanding provides a gentle and quiet spirit. Women are to respect their husbands. Men are to love their wives.

(b) How can you show greater love and respect to your husband this week as a witness to him and others?

Personal response

(c) How should today's Christian wife differ from Vashti?

Unless there was something immoral or ungodly implied in her husband's request, she could easily have left her banquet with the ladies temporarily to make an appearance at her husband's social event.

―――――――――――――――――――――――――――――― Day 3

7. **Read Esther 1:13–18.**

It was customary in this time that the king's word was considered law and could not be broken. What impact could Queen Vashti's response have had on the entire community?

It could cause the community to disrespect the king and choose to disobey his authority and the laws of the land in a way that could cause anarchy.

8.   How is Queen Vashti's behavior similar to the stumbling
        block Paul describes in Romans 14—particularly in
        verse 13?

        Her example was the standard by which the women of the king-
        dom behaved. In other words, they took their cue from her, so
        her disrespect for her husband had far greater consequence
        than the actions of another. A more vulnerable woman who
        looked to Vashti for direction could be caused to stumble by dis-
        regarding her husband's leadership and causing needless dis-
        cord in her marriage.

9. (a) King Xerxes' counselors understood the times in which
        they lived. As a Christian woman today who under-
        stands the times in which she lives, list several actions
        you should avoid so as not to present a stumbling block
        to other women.

        Sample answers:
        Verbally malign your husband's character.
        Disregard your husband's requests or concerns.
        Scoff at your husband's ideas to others.

    (b) Pray now that God will enable you to be his witness to
        this generation.

─── DAY 4

10.   **Read Esther 1:19–20.**

        What was the desire and purpose of the decree (verse
        20)?

        All the women would respect their husbands.

11. (a) Look up the word *respect* in the dictionary and write the
        definition.

        To feel or show honor or esteem for, to show consideration for.

    (b) Read Ephesians 5:33 and describe ways wives show
        respect for husbands.

Mention your appreciation and gratitude for character qualities you see in your husband.

12. **Read Titus 2:3–5.**

(a) List three practical ways that you can personally apply this Scripture.

Sample answers:

To resist criticizing _____ this week.

Verbally express love to my husband and children both at home and in public by complimenting with genuine appreciation something they do or say.

Finish some unfinished projects at home that would make our home a more orderly place to live and which would help our family function more smoothly—organize cabinets, create a chart for the children to complete household chores that go undone, fold and iron the laundry piled in the basement, or plan a special meal just for fun.

(b) Pray that Jesus will fill you to overflowing with his Holy Spirit so you can find the joyous fulfillment of representing his Word and his life to those around you every day.

Personal response

══ DAY 5

13. **Read Esther 1:21–22.**

(a) "That every man should be ruler over his own household." Does this verse bother you?

Personal response

(b) Why or why not?

Personal response

14. Describe Jesus' care, concern, and position toward us as explained in the following verses.

1 Corinthians 11:3 The protective line of leadership, submission, and responsibility is woman cared for by man, who

willingly submits to Christ as Christ yields to the will of the Father joyfully.

Ephesians 1:22   Christ is responsible for the church.

Ephesians 5:21–33   Submit to one another out of reverence for Christ; while doing so the husband carries final responsibility for decisions made and actions taken, just as Christ remains responsible for the church.

Colossians 1:15–20   We as members of the church yield to the will and authority of Christ as he takes final responsibility for his church.

15. (a) How do Christ's submission to the Father and his headship over his body demonstrate a woman's position of submission as a protected one, freed from the heavy responsibility of final decisions and inevitable consequences?

God is gracious to allow us to function freely within the protective care of our husbands and of Christ's lordship. By his grace we do not have to carry the responsibility for the outcome of decisions. That rests with our husbands. The truly liberated woman enjoys the protective covering of her husband's leadership while becoming all Christ desires her to be. She enjoys the freedom of exploring the gifts, skills, and talents Christ has given her and of using them for his glory, honor, and praise.

(b) How does this freedom enable you to flourish, obediently following and serving your Lord as you explore the gifts and purposes God has for you?

While the husband carries the major responsibility for the work that provides financially for the family as seen in Genesis 3:17–19, the woman has the freedom to pursue God's will for her without shouldering this responsibility.

(c) Pray that God will show you his perspective on your cherished place as his woman.

Personal response

ESTHER 2

We see God's use of Mordecai and Esther in situations they never anticipated, in events of which they'd never dreamed. Both were in God's right place at the right time to fulfill God's right purpose. Esther, a Jew, became queen in preparation for God's plan for his people. God placed Mordecai in the position to uncover a murder plot and save the king. Neither Mordecai nor Esther, both Jews, would have ever had these opportunities in a foreign land except for the intervention of God.

This chapter teaches you how to say yes to God's sovereignty in situations beyond your understanding and over which you have no control. God is greater than any government, nationality, custom, or situation. You can trust his power and wisdom to care for you as you tackle all of life's difficulties. Are you trusting God today to act in your circumstances?

LECTURE SUMMARY

The first focus of this chapter is that of God's sovereignty to accomplish his purposes by ordering the circumstances and events of our lives.

The second is the training instilled by Mordecai as he prepared Esther for her place in history, and the similar training God desires that we extend to our children and those God has brought into our lives to be nurtured and taught.

Finally, we see the rewards of obedience as Esther yields to the wisdom and insight offered by those in authority over her, both Mordecai and Hegai. God honors those who yield to him as they accept the instruction of those he has placed in their lives to guide them.

$=$ DAY 1

1.   **Read Esther 2:1–10.**

      What do you learn of Esther's and Mordecai's personal backgrounds from the passage?

      Esther
      Beautiful young virgin
      Named Hadassah or Esther
      Lovely in form and features
      Adopted by Mordecai when her parents died
      Brought to the citadel of Susa, placed under the care of Hegai
      Pleased Hegai and won his favor; he immediately provided her with beauty treatments and special foods
      Was assigned seven maids and moved to the best place in the harem
      Concealed her Jewish heritage, as Mordecai had insisted

      Mordecai
      A Jew of the tribe of Benjamin
      Son of Jaor
      Carried into exile from Jerusalem by Nebuchadnezzar, king of Babylon
      Had an orphan cousin, Esther, whom he raised

2.   "When the king's order and edict had been proclaimed, many girls were brought to the citadel of Susa." This was not a matter of choice or option. Neither Esther nor Mordecai could do anything about it. In many countries today Christians are finding themselves in similar circumstances. How do the following verses give instruction to Christians who live under government dictatorship?

      Matthew 28:18   God uses circumstances such as Esther's to fulfill his commission that we go to all nations.

Romans 13:1–7   Submit to governing authorities because God establishes them and you can entrust yourself to him in their midst.

Colossians 1:16–17   Thrones, rulers, powers, and authorities were created by God and he is sovereign over them.

1 Timothy 2:1–6   Make requests, prayers, intercession, and thanksgiving for kings and all those in authority that we may live peaceful and quiet lives in godliness and holiness.

Titus 3:1–2   We are to be subject to rulers and authorities, to be obedient and ready to do whatever is good, to slander no one, to be peaceable, considerate, and to show true humility.

1 Peter 3:21–22   Angels, powers, and authorities are in submission to God.

3. (a) Are there any areas in your life where you are tempted to resist the authorities set over you?
   Personal response

   (b) Respecting authority displays a good testimony for Christ and, even more, exhibits your faith in God's sovereign ability to care for you in every circumstance. Ask God to give you a willing heart to see those in authority in your home, church, and work as under his sovereign supervision, able to be used by him to bless your life.
   Personal response

═══════════════════════════════════════ DAY 2

4.   **Read Esther 2:11.**
      Why would Mordecai behave in such a manner?
      He loved her as a father and was concerned for her well-being.

5.   As a parent, grandparent, or one who cares for children, what are God's directions regarding your relationship with the child God places in your life?

      Deuteronomy 4:9   Teach what you have learned about God to your children.

Deuteronomy 6:7   Impress God's commandments on your children, talking about them always.

Psalm 78:1–7   Tell your children the praiseworthy deeds of the Lord. Remember his power and the wonders that he has done, causing them to put their trust in the Lord, remember his deeds, and keep his commands.

Proverbs 20:7   Our children are blessed when we live a righteous life dependent on Christ's righteousness and power.

Isaiah 49:15–16   In the same way that a mother cannot forget her children, God has us engraved on the palms of his hands.

Isaiah 66:13   God comforts us in the same way that he desires we comfort our children; our comfort will be a testimony to him.

Matthew 18:2–6   Jesus' tenderness and regard for children is an example as we deal with our children.

Ephesians 6:4   Fathers are not to exasperate their children but instead bring them up in the training and instruction of the Lord.

6.   Do you regularly show love and concern for your children or grandchildren, spending time with them and inquiring about their day and the needs of their hearts? Ask God for a sensitive heart to be aware of your children's needs and for wise words to encourage and minister to them.

Personal response

=== DAY 3

7.   **Read Esther 2:12–18.**

From verses 12–14, describe the extensive regimen Esther had to endure. What were her probable anxieties and how might her trust in God have been tested and strengthened during this period?

Esther had to endure twelve months of beauty treatments. Her anxieties might include: the fear of her nationality being discovered, the jealousy of the other virgins since she had been given a prime place, approaching the king, and the king's possible rejection. She had no one but the Lord to trust, forcing her to place these anxieties in his hand, her faith strengthened daily as she did so.

8. (a) Why is verse 15 significant in light of verse 13?
   Anything she wanted was hers to take when meeting the king but she chose only to take the things Hegai suggested, reflecting the respect for authority she had learned as a child from Mordecai.

   (b) How did God honor Esther's simple obedience?
   By simply following Hegai's suggestion she won the king's heart.

9. (a) List ways you can obey God and bring him honor.
   Personal response

   (b) Pray now and ask God to help you read and obey his Word, that you might daily be transformed into his godly woman.
   Personal response

─── DAY 4

10. **Read Esther 2:19–23.**
    (a) What do you learn about Esther's character from verse 20?
    She continued to follow Mordecai's instructions as she had done when he was raising her.

    (b) King Xerxes' death could have greatly threatened the Jewish people. How did God use Esther in verses 21–23 to keep his plans from being hindered?
    When Mordecai discovered the plot, Esther reported it, giving the credit to Mordecai. The would-be assassins were killed.

(c) Ask God to give you a heart that hears and obediently responds to his Word in your situation today. God alone knows how your decisions and actions will later affect your family, friends, and even all of history.
Personal response

─── Day 5

11.   Trusting God's sovereign, caring love in all circumstances, including those over which we have no control, enables us to obey him willingly. He is able to reveal his character of faithfulness, wisdom, and power to us in and through every situation. Jesus himself obeyed the Father willingly (John 6:38). What do we learn of personal obedience to the will of God from these verses?

Job 22:21   Submit to God and be at peace with him.

Psalm 40:8   Our desire is to do his will, to keep his law within our hearts.

Matthew 7:21   Our desire should be to do the will of the Father who is in heaven.

Ephesians 4:1–6   Live a life worthy of the calling we have received.

James 4:15   Yield to the Lord's will in everything.

1 Peter 4:2   Live your earthly life for the will of God.

1 John 5:14   When we pray, we should pray first to know his will so that as we pray according to his will he will hear us and our desires will be met.

12.   What is God's will for you? Discover it in these verses and pray that God will encourage you daily to walk in his will.

Acts 20:27   That I know the "whole will of God" as found in God's Word.

Romans 11:33–12:2   That I offer myself as a living sacrifice, holy and pleasing to God and that I refuse to be conformed to the world's pattern but be transformed by the mind's renewing. Then I will be able to test and approve what God's will is—his good, pleasing, and perfect will.

Ephesians 5:15–20   That I understand what the Lord's will is by living wisely, making the most of every opportunity, refusing drunkenness, which leads to debauchery. I can instead speak to others in psalms, hymns, and spiritual songs.

Philippians 2:12–13   That I yield to God's work in me to accomplish his good purposes.

1 Thessalonians 4:3–8   That I be sanctified, yielding to the process by which I am more completely molded into the image of his Son.

1 Thessalonians 5:12–22   That I respect those who work over me; that I live at peace with others; that I warn the idle, encourage the timid, help the weak; that I am patient with all, always joyful; that I pray continually and give thanks in all circumstances.

ESTHER 3

Is worship a significant part of your life? As we see in this chapter, God takes worship seriously. Mordecai risks his life to preserve his right to worship God and God alone. In this chapter we will see the pride and arrogance of evil people as contrasted with the humility of someone who bows to God alone.

Saying yes to our faithful and trustworthy God amid the plots of evil people is the thrust of this study. Are you relying on the faithful character of God as you face unknown and often unwelcome situations each day in this fallen world?

LECTURE SUMMARY

In this study we will examine the passage from three vantage points. The first will be an overview of observations concerning the characters of Mordecai and Haman.

By evaluating their motivations, their attitudes about God, and their actions as a result of both, we will contrast the character qualities of a man or woman who seeks to honor God with those of someone who is driven by the opinion of people.

Second, we will consider worship. The dictionary definition of worship is "reverence or devotion, to adore, intense love or admiration for; greatness of character, honor, dignity and worthiness." Like the Jews, we are called to worship only God. How does our daily and weekly worship reflect that calling? John 4:24, Romans 12:1–2, and Acts 17:23 will provide the foundation for this emphasis.

Finally, God's power over the devices of wicked people will comprise our third focus point. This chapter graphically describes God's power to overcome the ways of the wicked and the schemes of the devil who directs their behavior. We remember the words of Job 42:2, "No plan of yours can be thwarted." This statement remains forever true. God's purposes will always be accomplished according to his will in our lives no matter how fierce the devil's opposition. No purposes of God will be stopped throughout all eternity.

== DAY 1

1.   **Read Esther 3:1–4.**

   (a) Why did Mordecai refuse to kneel to Haman?

   In this culture rulers and nobles were viewed as deities. They were to be worshipped as such. Mordecai refused to attribute honor, glory, or deity to any but his God.

   (b) Why do you think Mordecai reveals his Jewish identity at this point?

   Because through this he was able to acknowledge the God of his people the Jews, and in so doing give glory to his name.

   (c) How do the following Scriptures support Mordecai's refusal to obey this particular authority over him?

   Exodus 20:1–5   "You shall have no other gods before me." "You shall not make for yourself an idol in the form of anything. . . . You shall not bow down to them or worship them. . . ."

   Exodus 23:24–26   "Do not bow down before their gods or worship them or follow their practices."

   2 Kings 17:35   "Do not worship any other gods or bow down to them, serve them or sacrifice to them."

2.   What do you learn from these verses about God's view of honor and worship?

1 Chronicles 16:29   God desires that we "ascribe to the LORD the glory due *his* name."

Psalm 9:1–2   God desires that we praise him.

Psalm 95:6   God desires that we bow down and kneel before him offering the worship due his name.

Psalm 100:2–3   God wants us to worship him with gladness and joyful songs, recognizing that he made us and that we belong to him.

Isaiah 46:9   We are to remember that he alone is God and there is no other.

Daniel 3:4–28   We are to bow down and worship God alone.

3. (a) Do you regularly attend church worship service? When you attend do you genuinely worship God, praising him for who he is and giving him the honor and glory due his name?

Personal response

   (b) Ask yourself if you place anyone or anything—status, perfectly decorated home, extravagant car, designer clothes, education, intelligence, a pastor, a friend—at a higher priority than God would desire. Pray now for God's perspective.

Personal response

   (c) Read the following verses and ask God to show you how to worship him, Lord God Almighty, above all else.

John 4:24   Worship flows from the spirit, soul, and heart of the believer. It is not an empty ritual nor has it a set form to be followed constantly. It is a heart response of love for God that is based in and extends out of a knowledge of the truth about God and the truth of his Word.

Acts 17:24   God is spirit and lives within the believer. We build buildings where we join to worship him, but he is not in the cement and bricks of the buildings. He is present as he indwells the life of every believer.

Romans 12:1–2   Our spiritual act of genuine worship is to again give our bodies and lives to God as a sacrifice of love for him to use for his glory, honor, and praise as he conforms us into the image of his Son.

═══════════════════════════════════════ DAY 2

4.   **Read Esther 3:5–6.**

What character qualities do you see in this passage that led to Haman's eventual undoing?

Pride, arrogance, hatred, jealousy, vengeance

5.   What are God's thoughts on the pride and jealousy seen in these verses?

God hates pride. It opposes the truth of his character as God and stands in opposition to all that God is.

6.   (a) Identify an area in your life where you are tempted to be proud.

Personal response

(b) Are you jealous of anyone's position, possessions, or presence today? Ask God to deliver you from pride and jealousy and from their consequences.

Personal response

(c) Ask God to help you humbly depend on him for his perfect plans for your life. Read Philippians 2:1–11.

Personal response

═══════════════════════════════════════ DAY 3

7.   **Read Esther 3:7–11.**

(a) How does Haman describe the Jews to Xerxes in verse 8?

Their customs are different from those of all other peoples.

They do not obey the king's laws.

It is not in the king's best interest to tolerate them.

(b) How is Haman described in verse 10?

As "the enemy of the Jews"

(c) Haman was not only arrogant and jealous, but a liar as well. What is God's perspective on lying, as seen in these passages? Search the Scriptures for other references about lying and its consequences.

Psalm 63:11   Liars' mouths will be silenced.

Proverbs 19:9   He who pours out lies will be punished.

Colossians 3:9–10   We are commanded not to lie to each other.

1 John 2:21–22   No lie comes from the truth.

(d) God tells us to speak the truth in love (Ephesians 4:15). Are little white lies permissible? Why or why not?

They do not exist.

There are no white lies.

Either something is a lie or it is truth.

"Bending the truth" is lying.

8.   Pray now and ask the Holy Spirit to reveal any lies you have spoken to anyone. Confess these as sin and ask God to cleanse you, empowering you to speak truth-fully in all things from this time forward. Claim God's promise in 1 John 1:9, confessing each time this happens and determining again by God's power to habitually walk in truth.

Personal response

=== DAY 4

9.   **Read Esther 3:12–15.**

Only an evil mind could devise such an act of vengeance. Have you ever wondered how people think of such evil deeds? From these passages list phrases that help you discover God's explanation for this.

Romans 1:18–32   They know the truth about God but suppress it and their outcome is that God's wrath will be poured out against them.

Romans 8:6–7   The sinful mind is hostile to God; it does not, nor is it able to, submit to God's law; those controlled by the sinful nature cannot please God.

Ephesians 4:17–19   Futile in their thinking; darkened in their understanding; separated from the life of God; hearts are hardened; indulge in every kind of impurity and lust for more.

10.   What can you do to develop a clean, pure thought life, pleasing and honoring to Jesus Christ? Study these passages and write phrases which give you direction in developing such a thought life.

1 Chronicles 28:9   Acknowledge the Lord; serve him with wholehearted devotion and with a willing mind; seek him and he will be found.

Isaiah 26:3   Trust the Lord and keep your mind steadfastly on him.

Matthew 22:37   Love the Lord with all your heart, soul, and mind.

Ephesians 4:20–24   Put off your old self; be made new in the attitude of your mind; put on your new self, created to be like God in true righteousness and holiness.

Philippians 4:8–9   Think on whatever is true, noble, right, pure, lovely, admirable, excellent, and praiseworthy.

11.   Personalize Romans 12:2 by prayerfully placing your name after each phrase as you read. Pray now that you will be "transformed by the renewing of your mind" as you seek God through your study of his Word.

Personal response

12.   Think back over the last two weeks of the study of the
       Book of Esther. List the qualities of human nature that
       have been revealed.
       Pride, arrogance, deceitfulness, hatred, vengeance, lying,
       judging

13.   **Read Psalm 64.**
       Note phrases that clearly identify the qualities of sinful
       humanity we have probed in Esther and phrases that
       portray God's sovereignty over the plans of evil people.

Qualities of Sinful Humanity	God's Sovereignty
Threatening	God will shoot them
Conspiracy	with arrows.
Noisy crowd of evildoers	They will be struck
Sharpen their tongues	down.
like swords	He will turn their own
Aim their words like deadly	tongues against them.
arrows	He will bring them to
Shoot from ambush at the	ruin.
innocent, suddenly and with-	All who see them will
out fear	shake their heads in
Encourage each other	scorn.
in evil plans	
Talk about hiding their snares	
Plot injustice	
Mind and heart are cunning	

14. (a) What is David's final proclamation in Psalm 64:9–10?
        Mankind will fear God and proclaim his works, pondering what
        he has done. The righteous will rejoice in the Lord, take refuge
        in him, and praise him.

(b) Can you thank God now for his sovereign care over you amid the difficult circumstances of your life, or the life of a relative or friend?

Personal response

(c) Pray now for God's comfort and strength. Ask God to increase your trust in him in all of life's circumstances.

Personal response

ESTHER 4

Haman plans the destruction of the entire Jewish nation. Esther, alarmed by Mordecai's anguish, inquires as to his distress. He tells her everything and then challenges her to take an action that could cost her her life, making her a sacrificial offering for the preservation of God's people. Can she believe God and risk her very life for the sake of his people? Saying yes to God in spite of natural human fear is the focus of this study. Is fear dominating and controlling your life, or is trust in God replacing that fear daily?

LECTURE SUMMARY

Answering the question "Who do you turn to in time of trouble?" provides the focus for this passage. Mordecai refused the compromise of accepting the temporary comfort offered by Esther and chose to seek the permanent comfort found only in the providential care of God. Mordecai's sackcloth and ashes would not be replaced by anyone but God, and he trusted him above all others. Who do you turn to in times of trouble? Do you seek the temporary relief of human touch or the permanent reprieve of God's intervention?

Second, we will focus on Mordecai's program for suffering. He began with prayer, followed with preparation, and then instituted a plan. In times of suffering are you sensitive to the Holy Spirit's direction as to an action you are to take? Mordecai was ready when Esther's eunuch came inquiring about the problem. He prayed, prepared himself with the necessary facts, and formulated a plan.

Third, we will see the truth that faith alone replaces fear. Esther's fearful response was replaced by an action of faith. She recognized her total dependence on God to work on her behalf and on behalf of her people; she stepped out in faith, approaching the king only after she knew everyone was praying and trusting God alone for the outcome. She depended not on the natural ways of people, but on the supernatural works of God. Where is your reliance today as you face times of suffering and distress?

—————————————————————————————— DAY 1

1.   **Read Esther 4:1–3.**

(a) What was Mordecai's first response upon hearing the edict?

He immediately went into mourning as symbolized by the wearing of sackcloth. He wailed loudly and bitterly. (When in anguish over sin and seeking the intervention of God, the Jew tore his clothes and put on sackcloth and ashes.)

(b) To whom did he turn?

The Lord

(c) How did the Jewish people respond?

They, too, pleaded with the Lord in mourning over this great grief that had befallen them.

2.   (a) When you face a difficult, possibly life threatening occurrence, whom do you turn to first?

Personal response

(b) List on a separate sheet of paper the individuals mentioned in Hebrews 11:7–40. Beside each name describe the circumstances referred to in the verses, the individual's action and attitude, and God's response.

Individual	Circumstances	Action	Attitude	God's Response
Verse 7, Noah	Was warned about the flood	Built the ark	Faith	Made him heir of righteousness
Verse 8, Abraham	Called to an unknown land	Obeyed and went	Faith	Made him heir of God's promise
Verse 11, Abraham	He was too old and his wife was barren	Believed the promise	Faith	Provided the heir whose descendants were the people of God
Verse 17, Abraham	Tested by God	Obeyed	Believed God	Provided another sacrifice
Verse 20, Isaac	Jacob and Esau competed for the blessing	Blessed them both	Faith	Gave both the future accordingly
Verse 21, Jacob	Dying	Blessed Joseph's sons and worshiped	Faith	Honored his prayers for future generations
Verse 22, Joseph	Close to death	Spoke of the exodus and his burial	Faith	Fulfilled prophecy of the exodus and Joseph's bones buried accordingly
Verse 23, Moses' parents	King's edict that all male children of certain age be killed	Hid him	Faith	Used Moses to deliver his people and direct them to his promised land
Verse 24, Moses	Lived in the king's house in a pagan nation	Chose to be mistreated with the people of God rather than enjoy the king's luxuries	Faith	Used Moses for his glory
Verse 27, Moses	Israelites enslaved to the Egyptians	Left Egypt not fearing the king	Faith	Delivered his people as a type of the deliverance his Son would bring to all
Verse 29, Israelites	Pursued by Egyptians	Passed through the Red Sea	Faith	Drowned the Egyptians, saving his people
Verse 30, Israelites	Told by God to conquer Jericho	Marched around the walls as God instructed	Faith	Tumbled the walls of Jericho to the ground
Verse 31, Rahab	God's spies came	She hid and protected them	Faith	Saved her life

3. (a) How is faith defined in Hebrews 11:1, 6?
       "Faith is being sure of what we hope for and certain of what
       we do not see." Believing that God exists and rewards those
       who trust him is faith that pleases God.

   (b) Describe *faith* in your own words.
       Personal response

   (c) Ask God to increase your faith (Luke 17:5) as did the
       disciples and pray today for the Holy Spirit's enabling
       to turn first to God in all the events of life.
       Personal response

=== DAY 2

4.   **Read Esther 4:4–5.**

      What was Esther's first response when she heard of
      Mordecai's activities?
      Distress and concern for him

5.   What was Jesus' response to the needs of those around
      him as recorded in these passages?

      Matthew 9:36   Compassion
      Matthew 14:14   Compassion
      Mark 1:41   Compassion
      2 Corinthians 1:3–4   Compassion and comfort
      Colossians 3:12   Compassion, kindness, humility, gentleness,
      patience

6. (a) How does Esther's sensitivity illustrate godly char-
       acter?
       By his Spirit God alone gives us the qualities that reflect his per-
       son and are alien to our own selfish human natures.

   (b) How does it reveal God's preparation of her heart to
       face her circumstances?
       Only as she was sensitive to the Holy Spirit and exemplified the
       qualities of God's character would she be able to approach the

king uninvited and live—God prepared her faith in him before she attempted such an action.

(c) Thank God today for using all the events of your life to help you become his woman.

Personal response

(d) Thank God for his promise for you found in Romans 8:28–29.

All things are working for good to conform us into the image of God's Son.

=== DAY 3

7.   **Read Esther 4:6–8.**

(a) What phrases show that Mordecai had diligently prepared for Esther's inquiry?

Told everything that had happened to him.

Knew the exact amount of money that Haman promised to pay the royal treasury.

Gave a copy of the edict which had been published in Susa to Hathach.

Apparently explained the document to Hathach so he could in turn explain it to Esther.

Told Hathach to urge Esther to go into the king's presence begging for mercy for her people.

(b) Did Mordecai's sackcloth and ashes represent despair and hopelessness, or was Mordecai believing God for a plan greater than the enormity of the situation?

Mordecai's faith was in God to accomplish the impossible.

8.   When you face difficult situations in life, what is your first reaction? Do you turn first to God, or is your response one of hopelessness, defeat, and self-pity? How would you like to react?

Personal response

9.   **Read Deuteronomy 10:17–21; Psalm 47; 103:11–19; Jeremiah 32:17.**

Ask God to forgive you for despair and unbelief, and to strengthen you with the realization that he is fully in control of all things, able to act in power on your behalf on all occasions. He loves you and desires only the best for you. Trust him today for his perfect will for your life as you identify any personal problems.

Personal response

―――――――――――――――――――――――――――――――――― DAY 4

10.   **Read Esther 4:9–11.**

(a) What normal and genuine human emotion was Esther experiencing at this moment?

Fear

(b) Are you ever afraid? Is fear a sin?

Fear is not a sin. It is an emotion God gives us for self-protection. It only becomes a tool of sin when we let it motivate our actions and keep us from doing God's will. Disobedience to God's Word and will is always sin.

11. (a) How does God want us to deal with fear?

Pray and trust him with the situation that is causing fear.

(b) Discover God's perspective on fear in the following verses, and look for others in the Bible.

Psalm 23:4   God is our Shepherd so our trust in him replaces fear.

Psalm 34:4   God delivers us from all our fears when we seek him and ask him to do so.

Psalm 46:1–7   God is with us. He is our refuge and strength; therefore we will not fear.

Psalm 91   The God in whom we trust is our refuge and fortress—we need not fear.

Mark 5:36   Jesus tells us that belief replaces fear.

John 14:27   The peace only Jesus gives is the solution to fear.

12. (a) The Scriptures tell us to fear the Lord. What benefit do we derive from this?

Fear in this context means awe and reverence. We are to reverence and stand in awe of our God because he alone is the great and mighty God.

(b) List aspects of this fear found in these verses.

Deuteronomy 31:12–13   It is something to be learned.

2 Chronicles 26:5   He was instructed in the fear of the Lord and as long as he sought the Lord, God gave him success.

Psalm 19:9   It is pure, lasting forever.

Psalm 34:9   Those who fear the Lord lack nothing.

Psalm 111:10   It is the beginning of wisdom.

Psalm 147:11   The Lord delights in those who fear him, putting their hope in his unfailing love.

Proverbs 14:27   It is the foundation of life.

Proverbs 15:33   It teaches a person wisdom.

Proverbs 19:23   It leads to life, then one rests content, untouched by trouble.

Isaiah 11:2–3   The Holy Spirit makes the fear of the Lord possible.

(c) Choose one verse and pray that God will make it real in your life.

Personal response

== DAY 5

13.   **Read Esther 4:12–17.**

What meaning does Esther 4:14 have for your life as you desire to fulfill God's will and purposes in the generation in which he has chosen for you to live?

Personal response

14.   In verses 15–16 Esther depends completely on God.
        "Cast all your anxiety on him because he cares for you"
        (1 Peter 5:7). The essential element and powerful impact
        of God's people united in prayer is also exemplified in
        these verses: meditate on Philippians 4:6–7; Colossians
        4:2; and 1 Peter 3:12.

    (a) Are you willing to depend completely on God daily as
        you face the events of life?
        Personal response

    (b) Do you recognize the importance of your prayers as
        God works out his will for you?
        Personal response

    (c) Ask God to enable you to trust him fully. Pray faithfully
        that he might be glorified concerning the situations in
        your life.
        Personal response

ESTHER 5

There is no end to the greed and pride of the human heart without God. Haman exemplifies the worldly individual whose only desire is for riches, power, and glory. These qualities stand in stark contrast to the humility seen in the God who chooses to live with him who is contrite and lowly in spirit, the God who steps out of eternity into time in the person of his Son to die for the sin of the world.

Esther, on the other hand, is a woman of faith who risks everything for God's people and who exemplifies a gentle and humble heart. Chapter 5 focuses on saying yes to God in the face of persecution, while consistently demonstrating patience and perseverance. Are patience and perseverance qualities you'd like to exemplify? Use Esther's example as one you can follow in the situations that confront you this week.

LECTURE SUMMARY

Chapter 5 deals with three causes of emotional upheaval. The first is fear. Esther had genuine cause to fear. She expressed her fear and then, by depending on and trusting God, allowed faith to overtake her fear. Fear is not sin. Actions based on fear are sin because everything done without faith is sin. Esther made a request: gather all the Jews, fast and pray for me.

Mordecai obeyed the direction God placed on Esther's heart. He was a humble man and they were in this together. God honored their faith. Are you taking spiritual steps to conquer the fear in your life?

Not developing patience is the second cause for emotional upheaval in this passage. Learning to listen to God and to develop patience, and to wait on God's right timing, challenges us daily. *Patience* is defined as "possessing or demonstrating quiet, uncomplaining endurance under distress or annoyance." It is being "capable of tranquility while awaiting results." We see patience demonstrated in Jesus Christ's unlimited patience with Paul (1 Timothy 1:15–16). We are taught to clothe ourselves with patience (Colossians 3:12) and that patience is a fruit of the Holy Spirit (Galatians 5:22). We also learn that it is through faith and patience that we inherit all that is promised to us by God (Hebrews 6:12). Are you claiming God's promise for situations? Are you depending on the Holy Spirit's enabling power? Are you standing fully clothed with patience?

Finally, a third cause of emotional upheaval is persecution. All of us have been hurt by others inside and outside the church. God offers encouragement. He knows and understands. There is refuge in his presence. He gives instructions so that we occupy our time positively, not negatively, by seeking his face and depending on his deliverance.

His directions are clear. We are to bless those who persecute us by identifying positive qualities in the other individuals and commenting on them, showing mercy, with prayer that the Lord will work in their lives. We are not to let our hearts be troubled or to give in to fear. We are to love our enemies with God's supernatural *agape* love that flows from the Holy Spirit. God can give us the ability to recognize the insecurities, miseries, and other elements that cause our enemies to behave as they do, and make us willing to be his instruments of a forgiveness and love greater than humanly possible. Remember the mercy Jesus has shown you and pray that he will have mercy on them as well.

--- DAY 1

1.   **Read Esther 5:1–5.**

God honored Esther's faith of heart and action. The king "was pleased with her and held out to her the gold scepter that was in his hand." When the king's question came, Esther was not impulsive but was prepared with a plan—one requiring patience and perseverance.

(a) Are you patient in seeking God's purposes, waiting upon his timing and will?
Personal response

(b) Describe one incident where you acted impulsively and later regretted it.
Personal response

2.   What do you learn about patience from these passages?

Proverbs 25:15   Through patience a ruler can be persuaded.

Galatians 5:22   Patience is one element of the Holy Spirit's fruit.

Colossians 3:12   As God's chosen people, holy and dearly loved, this is one quality with which we are to clothe ourselves.

1 Timothy 1:15–16   God displays his unlimited patience because he continues his work of redemption in us even when we sin and fall short of his glory.

2 Timothy 4:2   With patience and careful instruction God's Word is to be preached so as to correct, rebuke, and encourage.

Hebrews 6:12   Through patience we inherit what God has promised us.

3. (a) Ask God to give you his patience as you deal with any specific situation in your life.
Personal response

(b) Pray now that his peace, "which transcends all understanding, will guard your hearts and your minds in Christ Jesus" (Philippians 4:7).
Personal response

4.   **Read Esther 5:5–8.**

Banquets are referred to thirteen times in the book of Esther. Esther used a banquet to prepare the king's heart for her request. How did this banquet show Esther's respect and appreciation for the king?

Sharing a meal in the Eastern culture represented the highest form of regard, intimacy, and fellowship. To have prepared such a meal and to invite the king and Haman to attend displayed friendship and appreciation. Jesus is referring to this intimacy in Revelation 3:20, a demonstration of the most intimate of relationships. In this Revelation passage it refers to Christ's literal indwelling of the believer.

5.   In these verses, what is God's view of banquets and feasting?

Deuteronomy 16:13–17   It is a time of celebration and joy.

Isaiah 25:1–9   It represents God's blessing on his people and his fond regard for them.

Matthew 22:1–14   It is a gift prepared by God to honor his Son.

Revelation 3:20   It represents the most intimate fellowship with Jesus.

6. (a) Do you prepare "feasts" that minister hospitality to strangers and the blessing of celebration to your family?

Personal response

(b) Joy and celebration are definitely parts of the Christian life. Prepare a feast of honor and celebration for someone in the coming weeks and do it as "for the glory of God" (1 Corinthians 10:31) that he might be pleased and glorified.

Personal response

7.   **Read Esther 5:9–10.**

Mordecai "neither rose nor showed fear in his [Haman's] presence." Mordecai was experiencing persecution solely as a result of his faith in God. Jesus instructs us that persecution is a real aspect of the Christian life. What can you learn about the persecution we face as Christians from these passages?

Matthew 5:10   It is a blessing to be persecuted for righteousness. The kingdom of heaven is the reward.

Mark 4:16–17   It can cause those whose commitment to Christ is insincere to be revealed.

John 15:20–27   The world persecuted Jesus; since we are not greater than he we can expect the same treatment.

Romans 8:35–39   No persecution will separate us from the love of God.

1 Corinthians 4:12–16   We will be persecuted but will always know that we are not abandoned. God is with us.

Galatians 6:12–16   We should expect and accept the reality of persecution, never choosing to escape it by denying the Lord or his will, found in his Word.

2 Timothy 3:10–17   Everyone who wants to live a godly life will be persecuted but God is able to rescue us from all persecution.

8.   (a) Is there someone who has persecuted you for your faith in Christ? Describe one incident where this has occurred.
     Personal response

     (b) What instructions are you given for your response to such persecution?

     Matthew 5:44–48   Love your enemies and pray for those who persecute you.

     John 14:27   God gives us supernatural peace. Our hearts are not to be troubled and we are not to be afraid.

John 16:33   Jesus has overcome the world so, again, we do not have to be troubled or afraid.

Romans 12:14   We are to bless and not curse those who persecute us.

9.   Ask God to help you live uncompromisingly for him, trusting him for his peace in the face of persecution.
Personal response

━━━━━━━━━━━━━━━━━━━━━━━━━━━━━━━━━━━━━━━ Day 4

10.   **Read Esther 5:10–13.**
   (a) What do we see Haman doing in this passage?
   Boasting with pride

   (b) Have you ever been tempted to boast about some accomplishment so others will think more highly of you?
   Personal response

   (c) Find out how God views that kind of boasting from these verses.

   1 Samuel 2:3   Do not speak with pride and arrogance.

   Psalm 5:5   God cannot allow the arrogant to stand in his presence.

   Romans 2:17–24   You dishonor God by disobeying his Word while bragging about your knowledge.

   1 Corinthians 1:26–31   God chose opposite things from those the world extols as the things that he values. Because of this they cannot be obtained except through God's provision. No one can boast in themselves for obtaining them—all boasting then must be in the Lord.

   Galatians 6:14   Our only boast is in the cross of Jesus.

   Ephesians 2:8–9   Our salvation comes as a gracious gift from God. We did not work for it, nor could we earn it, so we have nothing of which to boast.

   2 Timothy 3:1–2   Boasting represents a worldly and ungodly value system.

James 4:13–17   Boasting is evil.

1 John 2:16   Boasting of what one has and does comes from the world, not from God.

11. **Read 1 Corinthians 1:31.**

(a) Read the following verses and list ways that we can boast in the Lord.

Jeremiah 9:23–24   We can boast that we understand and know God who exercises and delights in kindness, justice, and righteousness on earth.

Psalm 34:1–3   We can extol, praise, glorify, and exalt the Lord, which represents godly boasting in him.

2 Corinthians 12:9   We can boast about our weaknesses for they provide an ideal opportunity for the displaying of God's power.

Galatians 6:14   We can always boast in the cross of Jesus.

(b) Ask God for the ability this week to tell others about him rather than about yourself. Boasting about God reaps eternal rewards.
Personal response

═══ DAY 5

12. **Read Esther 5:14.**

(a) Who gave Haman the idea to hang Mordecai?
His wife and friends

(b) Consider your influence on the lives of those closest to you—your family, friends, neighbors, coworkers. Are you a godly influence on them?
Personal response

(c) Do you point others toward Jesus, or do you search for quick solutions and easy answers to their problems and needs?
Personal response

(d) What do you learn from these verses about the influence a woman has?

Genesis 3:1–20   Women have a great influence on their husbands.

Ruth 3:10–13   When women choose to obey him, God honors their obedience and their love is rewarded.

Proverbs 11:16, 22   Putting a valuable gold ring in an ugly pig's snout is as ridiculous as a beautiful woman who has no discretion; a kind-hearted woman gains respect.

Proverbs 21:9, 19   A quarrelsome woman or ill-tempered wife makes life miserable.

Proverbs 27:15–16   A quarrelsome wife is a terrible annoyance that cannot be stopped.

Proverbs 31:30   The woman who fears the Lord is to be praised.

Matthew 15:28   God honors a woman of faith.

Mark 14:3–9   The gift given from her heart made this woman an example for all generations.

Luke 1:26–38   Mary's faith in God's abilities and her desire to obey him caused her to be an example throughout all generations.

John 4:39   The woman's testimony caused many to believe in the Lord.

13. (a) Choose one verse that has particularly impressed you in this week's study. Write it here.
Personal response

(b) Explain its meaning for you personally and ask God to use his Word in this verse to transform your mind and heart this week.
Personal response

ESTHER 6

It's impossible to know the many ways God is supernaturally acting on our behalf throughout each day. Chapter 6 dramatically illustrates this fact as we see King Xerxes' sleeplessness coupled with his reading of the chronicles mentioning Mordecai's deed. There is no coincidence, only supernatural orchestration of events and times by God.

Before Esther could serve the next banquet, Haman was prepared to kill Mordecai. Esther could not know that, but God did. So he awakened the king and inspired his reading. Can God do the same for you today? Absolutely. Do you expect him to? I hope so. I hope you are always anticipating the intervention of God on your behalf.

The focus of our study this week is saying yes to God in faith and trust when faced with impossible obstacles. Watch closely as you see the ways the will of God is woven in and through every element of your life.

LECTURE SUMMARY

The first section of this text contrasts patience and humility to pride. Patience is rooted deeply in a trust of God. We as Christians are such "doers." We realize we cannot do anything apart from him. Waiting and trusting is founded on the knowledge that we are incapable of fulfilling God's will in our own strength. It is rooted in a trust that God is able to do more than we ask or think when we rely completely on him.

Humility is the state or quality of being humble. It is an absence of pride or self-assertion. Being humble means that one is aware of one's shortcomings and defects. The fruit of humility is a recognition of our inability as contrasted with God's capability (John 15:5; 2 Corinthians 12:9). Self-assertion versus God-assertion is the issue. The result of prideful self-reliance rather than humble God-dependence is stress. Stress results from self-promotion while the result of God-dependence and promotion in every area of life is peace and rest.

The second aspect for discussion in this passage is that of God's faithfulness toward the Jews (1 Chronicles 16:8–36). God's consistent faithfulness never varied. We see the testimony of his faithfulness spoken by Haman's wife. "Since Mordecai, before whom your downfall has started, is of Jewish origin, you cannot stand against him—you will surely come to ruin!" (Esther 6:13).

Faithfulness implies the continued, steadfast adherence to a person or thing. God promises to remain faithful toward his people for all time and eternity. This faithfulness is a constant, enduring, living testimony to all forever.

Finally, we will focus on faith. Using Hebrews 11, we see that God desires and extols faith exemplified in the lives of his people. Passages that can be studied and discussed on this topic include Luke 7:2–10; 17:5; 22:32; Romans 1:17; 3:3; and 4:19–21.

== DAY 1

1.   **Read Esther 6:1–3.**
     There are no coincidences with the Lord. He orders time and events. How do you see this illustrated in this passage?
     God awakened Xerxes and directed him to read the chronicles reporting Mordecai's action on his behalf.

2.   How are the following incidents similar to this scene in Esther 6?

Genesis 41:1–45   God gave Pharaoh a dream that needed Joseph's interpretation, getting Joseph out of the dungeon.

Daniel 2:1–23; 6:6–23   God gave Nebuchadnezzar dreams that brought Daniel to a place of influence that God used to witness of his greatness to a pagan nation.

3. (a) When situations seem overwhelming and solutions seem impossible in your life, do you trust God for the impossible and supernatural?
Personal response

(b) When all our resources are depleted, God is able. Take his promise in Ephesians 3:20–21 and ask him to stretch your faith and increase your trust for one specific impossible situation in your life today.
Personal response

=================== DAY 2

4. **Read Esther 6:4–9.**

What irony do you see in this situation?
Not only did Haman's pride dictate that honor be bestowed on the very man he planned to hang, but then he was selected to bestow the honor.

5. What do you discover in these verses about God's dealings with the wicked?

Genesis 13:13; 19:4–29   God destroys the evil one who wickedly sins without repentance against the Lord.

Psalm 1:5–6   The wicked will not stand with the righteous when God judges humanity.

Psalm 36   The evildoers lie fallen—thrown down, not able to rise.

Psalm 37:12–13   The Lord laughs at the wicked because he knows their day is coming.

Psalm 146:9   The Lord frustrates the ways of the wicked.

Proverbs 10:28; 11:5, 21   The hopes of the wicked come to nothing. The wicked are brought down by their own sin; the wicked will be punished.

6.   As the activities of wicked people surround us, our hope can rest in our sovereign God who knows all and is in control. The acts of the wicked do not surprise him.

(a) List six elements of wickedness today that threaten our culture, our communities, or our homes.

1. Pornography

2. Dishonesty in politics, business, the church

3. Influences of ungodliness in the media

4. Slander and gossip incited by journalism

5.

6.

(b) Pray that God will defeat the wicked in each of these and grant members of your family his presence and protection as they seek to do his will.
Personal response

=== DAY 3

7.   **Read Esther 6:10–11.**

God not only honored Mordecai but he showed his faithfulness to his people, the Jews, whom Mordecai represented. God was glorified because his will clearly triumphed over Haman's wickedness. God's sovereign power to control all of life's events, including the results, is proclaimed.

(a) Are you going through a difficult time? As you are faithful in your walk with God, what are his promises to you?
Personal response

(b) What aspects of this truth touch your life? Thank God for his tender love for you!

Personal response

(c) Choose one of these verses that is particularly mean-ingful to you and meditate on it.

1 Samuel 2:8   God raises the poor from the dust, lifts the needy from the ash heap, seats them with princes, and has them inherit a throne of honor.

Psalm 31   God leads and guides, delivers, rescues, frees from traps, is a refuge, holds our times in his hands, bestows his goodness on those who take refuge in him, shelters and keeps safe, hears the cry for mercy, preserves the faithful, pays back the proud in full.

Psalm 84:11   God bestows favor and honor; withholds no good thing from those whose lives are blameless.

Zephaniah 3:17   God is mighty to save, takes great delight in us, quiets with his love, rejoices over us with singing.

John 12:26   The Father honors the one who serves Christ.

DAY 4

8.   **Read Esther 6:12–14.**

(a) To whom and to what does Zeresh attribute Haman's impending downfall?

Mordecai's Jewish origin

(b) How do her words acknowledge God's almighty power?

God's blessing toward his chosen people had been seen throughout the ages.

9.   **Read Isaiah 45:18–25.**

How does God's Word speak to Haman's situation?

All who rage against the Lord will come to him and be put to shame, "But in the Lord all the descendants of Israel will be found righteous and will exult."

10. **Read Romans 8:31–39.**

    (a) Reflect on the greatness of the almighty God, your Father through Jesus Christ, and appreciate the change-less value of his commitment to you.
Personal response

    (b) Write a prayer here thanking God for his eternal care for you.
Personal response

─────────────────────────────────── **DAY 5**

11. (a) What have you learned about God's character from this week's study?
Personal response

    (b) Choose one verse from this week's lesson that reflects an aspect of God's character for which you are especially grateful and write it here.
Personal response

    (c) Define this attribute in your own words.
Personal response

12. List five ways this attribute of God affects your life on a personal basis and in your relationships with others.

Sample answer:

God is faithful.

    1. I can trust God concerning my unbelieving husband. I believe God is actively working in his life and as I pray, he will be drawn closer to him.

    2. I can trust God to work his perfect will in my daughter's life even though her situation at school is difficult this year.

Personal response

ESTHER 7

Discretion and wisdom accompanied Esther as she approached the king. Haman received the just consequences for his evil plot against the Jews when he was hanged on the very gallows he had created for Mordecai's death. God prevailed over the plans of wicked people.

The focus of this lesson is learning to say yes to God as he convicts us of sin and works to create godly character in our lives—qualities of humility, gentleness, and freedom from critical spirits and angry hearts. Do you think before speaking? Esther's example is one we can follow for a lifetime.

LECTURE SUMMARY

Areas of interest in this passage include communication with someone in authority. Esther chose her issues. She was unwilling to come to the king with trivial concerns, but instead came with important matters. When we approach our bosses or others in authority about important issues we should first pray, then speak concisely, humbly, and truthfully. Many a poor decision has been made because an issue was thoughtlessly presented rather than prayerfully considered.

Another aspect of discussion is that of God's victory over evil. Second Chronicles 20:15–17 highlights God's victory over Satan's evil plots and plans. Satan has already lost the battle against God and though his fate is sealed, it will soon be completed. People plot evil but God transforms it into good for his people. Dramatically seen in the Book of Esther, this reality holds true for us who believe as well.

━━━━━━━━━━━━━━━━━━━━━━━━━━━━━━━━━━━━━━ DAY 1

1.   **Read Esther 7:1–4.**

What attitude or attitudes can you identify in Esther's words: "If we had merely been sold as male and female slaves, I would have kept quiet, because no such distress would justify disturbing the king."
Humility.

2.   Look up the word *humility* in the dictionary. How would you define humility?
The state or quality of being humble; acts of self-abasement.

3. (a) Humility is a quality of great worth to God. It is also a quality often lacking in people today. Define God's view of humility as found in the following verses.

Proverbs 11:2   With humility comes wisdom but with pride comes disgrace.

Proverbs 15:33   Humility comes before honor.

Proverbs 22:4   Humility and the fear of the Lord bring wealth, honor, and life.

Philippians 2:3   In humility consider others better than yourself.

Titus 3:1–2   Rulers are to show true humility.

James 3:13–18   Humility comes from wisdom; humility is the opposite of envy and selfish ambition. Wisdom that brings about humility is pure, peace-loving, considerate, submissive, full of mercy and good fruit, impartial, and sincere.

    (b) Pray that God will reveal areas of pride or self-promotion in you. Ask for his forgiveness.
Personal response

(c) Ask God to give you a heart of humility so rarely found in our world but of such value to him.

Personal response

DAY 2

4.   **Read Esther 7:5–10.**

        Outline the story plot with verses that mark the events of this scene.

        Verse 5: Xerxes inquires who would plot to kill Esther's people.

        Verse 6: Esther exposes Haman.

        Verse 7: King stomps out in a rage. Haman stays behind to beg Esther for mercy.

        Verse 8: The king returns to find Haman near Esther and accuses Haman of molesting her. The executioners pull the bag over Haman's head even as the king speaks. Harbona, the king's servant, tells of the gallows Haman built to kill Mordecai and reminds the king of Mordecai's act to protect the king from assassins earlier.

        Verses 9–10: The king commands Haman be hanged on the very gallows Haman built for Mordecai.

5.   List all the events which came together at this time to condemn Haman.

        1. Haman builds gallows for Mordecai.

        2. Queen Esther exposed Haman's treachery.

        3. King became outraged.

        4. Haman fell at Esther's feet, giving the appearance of molestation.

        5. King re-entered and was incensed.

        6. Haman was hanged on the very gallows he had built.

6. (a) Esther waited patiently on the Lord for his perfect timing before speaking. She then spoke concisely, humbly, and truthfully. Explain how Esther's approach in this life-threatening situation is an example to God's people

when they approach employers, church leaders, and others in authority with concerns they consider serious.

It is always wise to think before speaking of important matters and to create an amiable environment conducive to listening and understanding before words are spoken. Esther did both of these things, I'm sure after much prayer. Do you seek the Lord before you speak about important business or family matters? As we consider the conversations and deliberations required throughout daily life, Esther's example can be helpful. Communication is the key to all relationships. Good communication skills can be developed and will prove to be an invaluable asset for a lifetime.

(b) List four ways you can apply a similar approach in the circumstances of your life today.

Personal response

DAY 3

7. In his book written specifically for men, *If Only He Knew,* Gary Smalley writes an aside to wives. "Wives, if you are reading this, let me assure you that we as husbands generally do not know what you need. So we ask you to help us learn by telling us your needs in a gentle, loving way. Let us know when we aren't meeting your needs—but not in critical ways that could cause us to lose interest." Esther could have stormed into King Xerxes' presence at any moment questioning him with words like, "How dare you . . . how could you sign that edict to kill all the Jews?" That would have been a fatal mistake. Gentle words bring healing and change. What are God's admonitions in these verses?

Proverbs 15:1   A gentle word turns away wrath, harsh words stir up anger.

Proverbs 25:11, 15   A word aptly spoken is like apples of gold in settings of silver; patience and gentle words can cause persuasion.

Matthew 12:36   Remember that people will have to give an account on judgment day for every careless word spoken.

James 1:19   Be quick to listen, slow to speak, and slow to become angry.

James 3:8–12   The tongue is a restless evil full of deadly poison—out of the same mouth come blessing and cursing—this should not be.

8.   **Read Psalm 141:3; Proverbs 13:3; 21:23.**

   (a) Can you think of a current relationship or situation in your life where you can apply these truths? Describe here.
   Personal response

   (b) Ask God to place a guard over your mouth and help you to gently speak words of truth and kindness.
   Personal response

═══ Day 4

9.   A critical mind-set that constantly attacks and condemns is an attitude we must avoid. Esther not only spoke gently, but avoided behaving harshly toward King Xerxes. What can you learn from the following verses concerning this attitude?

Colossians 3:12–17   Clothe yourselves with compassion, kindness, humility, gentleness, and patience. Bear with each other, forgiving all grievances you have against one another. Forgive as the Lord forgave you.

James 5:9–11   Do not grumble against each other or you will be judged; show patience in the face of suffering.

1 Peter 4:8–10   Love each other deeply because love covers a multitude of sins.

10. (a) Have you harshly criticized your husband, child, friend, or relative lately?
   Personal response

(b) Do you tend to see faults and shortcomings in others before you recognize their strengths?
Personal response

(c) Ask God to forgive you for any harsh attitudes that cause criticizing and accusing.
Personal response

(d) It takes thirty to sixty days to break a habit, psychologists report. Ask God's Holy Spirit to bring to your attention, for the next two months, every critical, negative thought or word about other people. Each time you are stopped short by the Spirit's reminder, try to replace the negative thought with a positive one. Ask forgiveness of the other person when harsh thoughts become critical words. Speak praise to replace criticism. Look for transformations in your life as well as in others' lives.
Personal response

DAY 5

11. Esther exemplified the character of a godly woman. Proverbs 31:10–31 continues to stand as a magnificent portrayal of godly womanhood. Read this passage and select the quality that you particularly desire for God to work into your life.
Personal response

12. (a) Write a prayer expressing your desire to the Lord.
Personal response

(b) Claim Philippians 1:6 and 2:12–13 as God's promise to you as you pray.
Personal response

ESTHER 8

God uses every event of life to accomplish his perfect purposes. Though the threat Haman posed jeopardized the Jews' lives, God heard their mourning and saw their fasting. He answered, not only by providing immediate deliverance, but by establishing future protection for them and their families.

God's ways are always best, and because of his omniscience he always works in light of a future only he can see. Truly deliverance came to the Jews and to the generations to follow, only one of God's many expressions of the complete deliverance he prepared through his Son.

Saying yes to the faithfulness of God concerning the relationships in our lives and trusting him to take care of the difficult people is the thrust of this week's lesson. When you are slandered and verbally abused, do you turn first to God? Learn how to rest in his control over your relationships and to depend on his watchful care.

LECTURE SUMMARY

In this section of Scripture, we will first discuss Esther's regard for her parent. She shows her respect for her adoptive father, Mordecai, by bringing him before the king to be honored and then by turning Haman's estate over to him for his care.

Next we see the positive impact a woman can have on her husband's life. Esther's complete dependence on God gave her the power to positively influence Xerxes' life in a way that brought God glory, honor, and praise.

Finally we see that God uses every situation to prove his faithfulness so that he might be glorified and others will be drawn to him. We, too, have the privilege of experiencing this partnership with God.

—————————————————————————————— DAY 1

1.   **Read Esther 8:1–2.**

      Who was Esther thinking of first when King Xerxes gave her Haman's estate?

      Mordecai, rather than herself

2.   Mordecai was Esther's adoptive father. Study the following verses and explain how Esther's action showed respect for God and his Word.

      Exodus 20:12   Honor your father and your mother.

      Proverbs 23:22   Listen to your father, who gave you life, and do not despise your mother when she is old.

      Matthew 15:3–9   Honoring one's mother and father is a command of God to be obeyed.

      Matthew 19:17–19   To experience the life God desires, honoring your father and mother is a commandment to be obeyed.

      Ephesians 6:1–3   That all may go well with you and that you might experience long life are the results of honoring one's mother and father.

3.   God reveals himself to us as our Father. He desires that the earthly relationship we have with our parents be a type. That is, it should represent our relationship with him as our loving parent. Are you doing all within your ability to honor your father and mother? Have you recognized the even greater love God has for you than any earthly parent can express? Discover your heavenly Father's love in these verses and thank him now for his personal, precious love for you.

Deuteronomy 32:6   God is my Creator who made and formed me and is worthy of my love and worship.

Psalm 27:10   The Lord receives me even if my parents forsake me.

Psalm 68:4–6   God is a father to the fatherless, the defender of widows; he sets the lonely in families, and leads forth the prisoners with singing.

Psalm 103:13–18   The Lord has compassion on those who fear him; he knows how I am formed and remembers my frailty, that I am dust; from everlasting God's love is with those who fear him, with those who keep his covenant and remember to obey his precepts.

Matthew 6:25–34   My heavenly Father will provide for me with even greater care than he does for creation; my heavenly Father knows what I need. If I seek his kingdom and righteousness first, the other things will be mine.

Romans 8:15–17   I received the Spirit of sonship by which I can cry to God, *Abba,* Father—"Daddy." I am God's child and heir.

—————————————————————————————— DAY 2

4.   **Read Esther 8:3–13.**

In this passage God performs what had seemed impossible. How was this accomplished without contradicting the earlier law of the king (Esther 3:10–14)?

The king's law created by Haman was overruled by Mordecai's edict. In that culture the king's law was never overruled. The impossible was accomplished.

5.   When we completely depend on the Lord, he accomplishes his purposes. Esther faced death twice—first in chapter 5 verse 2 and again in chapter 8 verse 4 when she wonders if the king will raise his scepter. Esther was not at the king's mercy, but instead was dependent on God's. What do we learn of God's mercy and faithfulness toward us from the following verses?

Deuteronomy 4:31   Our Lord is a merciful God who does not forget his covenant with our forefathers (which applies to all who believe in the Son). He will never abandon or destroy us.

Psalm 28:6   God hears my cry for mercy.

Lamentations 3:22–23   Because of the Lord's great love we are not consumed; his compassions never end.

Luke 1:50   From one generation to the next, his mercy goes on and on.

Ephesians 2:4   Because of his great love for us, God, rich in mercy, made us alive with Christ even when we were dead in transgressions.

Hebrews 2:9, 17–18   Jesus suffered death for us. He lived like us in human form so that he might be a merciful and faithful high priest, making atonement for our sins. Because he suffered when he was tempted, he understands our suffering when tempted.

6.   Thank God for his mercy toward you and apply John 15:5 to your life today, surrendering yourself fully to Jesus Christ, the Lord.

Personal response

═══ Day 3

7.   **Read Esther 8:9–14.**

The king's edict gave the Jews full right to protect themselves and beyond that "to plunder the property of" their enemies. They could show vengeance.

(a) Look up *vengeance* in the dictionary and define it here.

The return of an injury for an injury; in punishment or retribution; an avenging; revenge.

(b) Has anyone ever physically or verbally abused you?

Personal response

(c) Have you ever wanted to get back at or get even with someone?

Personal response

8.   Who alone has the right to vengeance? Study these verses, then write your answer in ten words or less.

Leviticus 19:18 Do not seek revenge, but love your neighbor as yourself.

Psalm 18:47 God avenges me.

Isaiah 34:8 The Lord has a day of vengeance.

Jeremiah 51:6, 11, 36 God will take vengeance.

Hebrews 10:30–31 The Lord will judge his people. Vengeance belongs to the Lord alone; we trust him.

9.   **Read Romans 12:19–21.**

Pray now for those you mentioned in question 7b and 7c, that they will be convicted of their sin and will turn to the living God! Pray also that you may be able to overcome their evil with good.

Personal response

=== **DAY 4**

10.   **Read Esther 8:15–17.**

An exciting moment takes place. Mordecai is honored by God and the people. God's triumph for his people is proclaimed. What is the result in verse 17?

Many people of other nationalities became Jews in response to God's action on behalf of his people.

11. (a) In *all* things God is glorified! He uses every circumstance in life to make himself known to us and to manifest himself through us. This causes the world to know that he alone is God and then to turn to him. Life is found in God alone, through Jesus Christ. As family, friends, neighbors, coworkers, and relatives watch your life, do

they see a testimony of God's faithfulness and power at work in and through you?
Personal response

(b) Pray now that you will grow bold in recognizing and acknowledging God's faithful presence in your life. Pray that you might be known as a vibrant follower of Christ.
Personal response

═══ DAY 5

12. The living God is aware of every aspect of your life. He knows and understands you better than you will ever know yourself. Obey God's Word; turn from sin and pursue him. You will have only the exuberant joy of knowing him and discovering life itself (John 10:10).

(a) Is there an area of your life you still cannot seem to give to God?
Personal response

(b) Are you nurturing sin that you imagine God is somehow unaware of?
Personal response

(c) What is causing you to hold back?
Personal response

ESTHER 9

God gave his people relief from their enemies, which was the intent of their fighting. Their fighting was defensive rather than aggressive and God protected them. Following God's deliverance from their enemies, celebration began. Rest, feasting, and joy marked the occasion in appreciation to God for his faithfulness.

Learning to say yes to God concerning his desire for joy and celebration in our Christian lives is the subject considered in this text. Is joy a prevailing aspect of your life? If not, why not? Find out God's perspective on joy in this week's study.

LECTURE SUMMARY

Faith conquered the Jews' fears. "No one could stand against them, because the people of all the other nationalities were afraid of them." God used the very fear of the other nations to the advantage of the Jews. The other people saw an awesome, unexplainable power of a God they did not know. God used this to protect his people and exalt his name. Daniel 3:13–30 demonstrates the power of God as seen through his people. When you are in a difficult circumstance, do people see God's power through you?

Celebrating God's deliverance supplies a second focus in the passage. Do you celebrate God's acts of kindness and deliverance toward your family in your home? How might you begin to do so?

Finally, our interests will turn to experiencing Jesus' joy. Joy is intended to be an integral part of the Christian life. We see this in Jesus' words in John 17. Do you feel guilty when you relax and experience joy? Why? Is this God's will for you or are you being robbed of the constant joy that is to be yours in Jesus? Are your or others' false attitudes or beliefs robbing you of joy? Identify and remove such attitudes today.

─── DAY 1

1.   **Read Esther 9:1–16.**
      Write the thought that comes to your mind as you read
      the following phrases:

The tables were turned
(verse 1).

The Jews got the upper hand
(verse 1).

> Those who thought they would kill and plunder the Jews were killed themselves.

No one could stand against
them (verse 2).

The people . . . were afraid of
them (verse 2).

> God inspired fear in the enemies of the Jews.

Fear of Mordecai had seized
them (verse 3).

> God was for Mordecai and that was recognized by all, causing them to fear.

His reputation spread throughout the provinces (verse 4).

He became more and more
powerful (verse 4).

> God honored Mordecai for his faithfulness to him and willingness to risk everything to protect his people.

They did what they pleased
to those who hated them
(verse 5).

> The Jews clearly had the victory.

They did not lay their hands on the plunder (verse 10).

The Jews were not greedy; their intent was to protect themselves from their enemies.

The Jews . . . assembled to protect themselves and get relief from their enemies (verse 16).

Self-defense was the driving force of their actions.

2.   Why do you think the Jews did not lay their hands on the plunder?

Because their interests were not selfish, they had no desire to debase or dishonor the work God had done on their behalf; it was a good sign to the inhabitants of other nations that they were not malicious and could be trusted.

3.   (a) The Jews defended themselves against those who hated them but they did not retaliate so as to exploit. Have you ever been attacked through an argument or gossip? Have you forgiven without retaliation, trusting God to work within the hearts and situations of those involved? When the truth became known, did you resist the desire to "plunder" the situation or the other person's reputation? Ask God to help you forgive those who have sought to harm you.

Personal response

(b) Pray that you might live your life before God as in Galatians 1:10, and trust him to take care of the opinions and judgments of those around you.

Personal response

━━━━━━━━━━━━━━━━━━━━━━━━━━━━━━━━━━━ DAY 2

4.   **Read Esther 9:17–22.**

How did the Jews respond to God's deliverance?

With joyous celebration and feasting

5. (a) An annual observance was ordered. What two reasons were given for the event?
   As a remembrance of God's deliverance and action that turned their sorrow into joy and mourning into celebration.

   (b) How was the day celebrated?
   Feasting, giving presents of food to one another and gifts to the poor.

6.   What celebrations do you observe as a family? Is the focus of each event thanksgiving to God for his blessing?

   (a) List your celebrations here.
   Personal response

   (b) Are there celebrations you need to eliminate because they are not God honoring?
   Personal response

   (c) Pray and ask God to help you identify events in which God has worked in your family's life that merit celebration. Plan one such celebration in the coming month.
   Personal response

=== DAY 3

7.   Joy and celebration are biblical concepts and yet many Christians seem joyless. From these passages, note causes for every Christian to rejoice.

   Nehemiah 8:10   The joy of the Lord is our strength.

   Psalm 16:11   We have joy in his presence.

   Psalm 149:4–5   Our joy flows from the fact that the Lord takes delight in us.

   John 15:11   The abiding presence of God in our lives is our source for joy.

   John 16:22–24   Joy springs from the fact that anything we ask in Jesus' name—in accordance with his will and character— is ours.

Ephesians 1:3–14   All the riches that are ours in Christ cause us to rejoice.

8.   Are you experiencing joy in Jesus Christ today? Pray today as David prayed, "Restore to me the joy of your salvation" (Psalm 51:12). Ask God to enable you to recognize his presence in your life and to fill you with his joy each day.

Personal response

─── Day 4

9.   **Read Esther 9:23–32.**

Describe the feast of Purim:

Its background   Haman in his plotting had cast the *pur*—the lot—for their destruction. But the plot came back on his own head.

Its purpose   To remember what they had seen—the tables turned—and what had happened to them—relief from their enemies.

Its manner of observance   They and their descendants would all celebrate these two days every year with joy and feasting, giving of presents, and giving to the poor.

10. (a) Describe your Christmas or Resurrection Day (Easter) celebration.

Its background   Personal response

Its purpose   Personal response

Its manner of observance   Personal response

(b) Ask God for three creative ways to make this celebration more Christ honoring and joyful for you and your family. Ask God to help you make your upcoming celebration one that is spiritually nurturing to your entire family and one to be remembered for years to come.

Personal response

11.   Review now the lives of the major characters in the Book of Esther. Fill in the following chart with phrases (and verse numbers when possible) that describe each aspect of their roles in Esther's drama.

	Actions Depicting Character	Major Role	How God Was Glorified
Vashti	Refuses to obey the king (1:12).	Makes way for Esther to become queen.	God's purpose was accomplished.
Esther	Obeys Mordecai (2:10).	She is in the right place at the right time.	Showed God's power to control circumstances.
	Approaches Xerxes in wisdom and humility.	Gains a hearing for the plight of the Jews.	Showed God's power over even tyrants.
Mordecai	Reports the assassins' plot. Reports Haman's plot.	Communicates to the king through Esther.	God's people, the Jews, got relief from their enemies.
King Xerxes	Rules as a despot; makes careless decisions in ruthless rage.	Accomplishes God's will though unaware.	God showed his supernatural power over the all-powerful king.
Haman	Hates Mordecai.	Plots the destruction of the Jews.	God's power over the wicked shown: Haman was killed and the Jews were exalted.

12.   Describe what you learned from each of these characters that you can apply in your own life.

   Vashti   Personal response

Esther   Personal response
Mordecai   Personal response
King Xerxes   Personal response
Haman   Personal response

13. (a) List the truths you've learned from studying the Book of Esther.
       Personal response

   (b) Ask God for continued growth in living in light of these truths. Share what you've learned with one other person this week.

ESTHER 10

Saying yes to God by placing him at the center of your life is the focus of this chapter. Do you order all of your priorities in a way that reflects your commitment to God as you seek to live out his will? Mordecai did. That is the example he leaves for us to follow in our walk with God. Learn more about your Christian commitment and the way it shapes your life.

LECTURE SUMMARY

This chapter's discussion is on glory. In Luke 2:14 we see God's proclamation throughout the ages, "Glory to God in the highest, and on earth peace to men on whom his favor rests." *Glory* is defined as "distinguished honor or praise; exalted reputation, or worshipful adoration." We will ask three questions. What is the glory of God? Where is it seen? What is our response?

What is the glory of God? John Piper in his book, *Desiring God*, describes God's glory as "the beauty of his manifold perfections. It can refer to the bright and awesome radiance that sometimes breaks forth in visible manifestations. Or it can refer to the infinite moral excellence of his character. In either case it signifies a reality of infinite greatness and worth." Exodus 29:42–46; Leviticus 9:23–24; Psalm 19:1; and Isaiah 6:3 demonstrate this truth.

Where is it seen? It is seen most perfectly in heaven because God is fully revealed there for every moment, past, present, and future. We are privileged to receive glimpses of his glory on earth as we seek his face and person. As we draw near to Jesus we experience the glory of the Triune God. Jesus' coming to earth revealed the glory of the Almighty, the complete representation of God's glory on earth.

What is our response? We are to "give Him the glory due his name." We reflect the glory of God as Jesus is revealed in us (Isaiah 43:6–7; 2 Corinthians 3:18). We are also to acknowledge his glory in all things (1 Chronicles 16:23–29; Luke 2:20).

Day 1

1. **Read Esther 10.**

   One person is honored in the chapter. Who is this person?

   Mordecai

2. For what will Mordecai be remembered for all time? (See verse 3.)

   He worked for the good of his people and spoke up for the welfare of all the Jews.

3. (a) If you were to die now, for what would you be remembered?

   Personal response

   (b) For what would you like to be remembered?

   Personal response

   (c) If your answers to (a) and (b) are different, ask God for his grace in your life to enable you to fulfill his purposes for you. Pray to become the person he desires you to be, accomplishing those things for which you have been placed in this generation.

4.   List at least five things you consider the priorities of your life.
     Personal response

5.   Now identify the top three priorities and place them in order of importance.
     Personal response

6.   On a separate sheet, briefly write your usual schedule for each day of the week, Sunday through Saturday.

   (a) How much time in the course of a day or week do you spend on the priorities you listed in question 5?
       Personal response

   (b) Are there changes you need to make?
       Personal response

   (c) Ephesians 5:15 speaks of "making the most of every opportunity," or in another translation, of "redeeming the time." Pray for wisdom to apply this in your life.
       Personal response

━━━━━━━━━━━━━━━━━━━━━━━━━━━━━━━━━━━ DAY 3

7.   Review the book of Esther in your mind. In your opinion, how can a book that doesn't mention God so obviously testify to his presence?
     God's sovereign orchestration of people, times, and events to accomplish his purposes is clearly seen.

8.   How do Paul's words in Romans 1:18–20 show another way God is made known without being mentioned?
     Through his creation he testifies to his presence and purpose to all people. It is irrefutable and anyone who refuses to yield to

God's lordship by pursuing wicked and evil practices is already condemned by his or her hardness of heart.

9.   The very existence of God is irrefutable, his presence undeniable. List ways God reveals himself to unbelievers and believers alike in our world today.
Sample answers:
The intricacies of his creation testify to his presence and creative power.
He provides for the needs of his people.
He sovereignly overrules the evil practices and ideals of political people who are ungodly.
He answers prayer and heals lives.

10. **Read Romans 1:21–32.**

(a) Do you know anyone who denies the existence of God?
Personal response

(b) What will be the outcome of his or her life without Christ?
Their thinking becomes futile and their foolish hearts are hardened.

(c) Pray for God's mercy and grace to abound in this individual's life, causing him or her to acknowledge Jesus Christ as Savior and Lord according to the truth found in Colossians 1:15–17.
Personal response

_____ DAY 4

11. **Read Esther 10:3 and Matthew 5:13–16.**
Pray for the boldness to lovingly speak God's uncompromising truth so that you might be salt and light in the world today.
By abiding in Christ and being sensitive to the Holy Spirit's guidance, we can be used by God for the advancement of his king-

dom and the glory of his name. We can do nothing in our power, but in his power God can accomplish miracles.

12.   What issues today demand that we promote a Christian perspective? List below.
Abortion
Euthanasia
Pornography, etc.

=== DAY 5

13. (a) How can you be a greater witness to those God has placed in your life?
Personal response

(b) Read the following verses. List the ways we can live worthy of the Lord and give a good testimony to the world.

Ephesians 4:1–7, 11–13   Be completely humble and gentle; be patient; bear with one another in love; by using the gifts God has given us for his glory .

Philippians 1:27–30   Conduct yourselves in a manner worthy of the Lord.

Colossians 1:9–14   Ask God to fill you with the knowledge of his will; live a life worthy of the Lord and please him in every way; be strengthened with the power of his glorious might.

14.   **Read John 15.**

Write a letter to God. Thank him for specific truths you have learned through this study of Esther. Ask him to conform you to the image of his Son (Romans 8:29) so that you can live a life of joy, bring him great pleasure, and live worthy of his wondrous name!
Personal response